GOVERNMENT SUPPORT FOR HIGHER EDUCATION AND RESEARCH

Other books by NIEPA

Education and the New International Order—*J. Veera Raghavan* (Ed.), 1983

Revitalising School Complexes in India—*R. P. Singhal*, 1983

GOVERNMENT SUPPORT FOR HIGHER EDUCATION AND RESEARCH

A Critical Study of Patterns, Procedures and Policies

J. L. AZAD

National Institute of Educational Planning and Administration, New Delhi

and

CONCEPT PUBLISHING COMPANY
NEW DELHI

The views expressed by the author in this publication, the selection of facts represented and the opinions stated with regard to the facts are the responsibility of the author and do not necessarily represent the views of NIEPA.

First Published 1984

Published by

Naurang Rai
Concept Publishing Company
H-13 Bali Nagar
NEW DELHI-110015 (India)

Printed by

Asia Composer
at Sunil Printers, Naraina
NEW DELHI-110028

TO MY MOTHER

WHOSE LIFE WAS A SAGA OF LOVE, DEVOTION AND SELF-ABNEGATION; WHOSE INDOMITABLE SPIRIT WAGED A RELENTLESS BATTLE AGAINST ADVERSITIES, THUS PROVIDING US AN ABIDING SOURCE OF INSPIRATION AND SUSTENANCE

AND

WHO WAS SNATCHED AWAY FROM US BEFORE HER DREAMS COULD TURN INTO REALITY.

MAY HER SOUL REST IN PEACE!

Foreword

EDUCATIONAL finance, as a subject for investigation, is fascinating as well as purposeful, not only because financial inputs are essential for the quantitative and qualitative development of education but also because rather scanty literature on this subject is available not only in this country but in the developed countries of the world as well. Furthermore, very few studies have been made to examine the patterns, procedures and policies of financing higher education and research adopted by the federal and the state governments in India. It is in this context that this attempt by Dr Azad to make an analytical study of the government support for higher education is most welcome.

The development of higher education in India in the post-independence period presents an interesting study in contrasts. There has been phenomenal expansion in the facilities for higher education. We can boast of institutions in the arts, sciences, engineering and technology and medicine, which can stand comparison with the best in the world. A large number of our university products are engaged in the most sophisticated and extremely complex operations requiring theoretical and practical competence of the highest order. The research papers produced at our centres of higher learning bear testimony to the competence of our research scholars. To have achieved this in a short span of less than four decades is an accomplishment of which we can justly be proud.

The debit side is, however, quite alarming. The quality of education in a number of institutions of higher learning leaves much to be desired. The exasperating escalation in the ranks of university educated who are unemployed, under-employed and unemployable speaks eloquently about the lack of adequate concern in the university system to the fast changing socio-economic complexion of this country. The outmoded, and in some cases, primitive curriculum in some disciplines may be cited as examples of the dysfunctional character of higher education in India. The mushrooming of institutions, quite a few of which are academically non-viable, is another phenomenon adding to the confusion in the system.

The complex problems in the sphere of higher education have been analysed by two high-powered commissions and a number of committees appointed by the central and state governments in the post-independence period. The various causative factors behind the apparently contradictory trends of excellence of the highest order and the mediocrity of the lowest level have been identified. While it would not be entirely correct to say that finance is the main cause of the malaise afflicting institutions of higher education, it would be naive to deny the importance of a good financial base for the development of higher education. It would, therefore, be quite instructive to assess the adequacy as well as role of the financial investment as well as policies adopted by the union and the state governments for the promotion of higher education.

It would also be pertinent to subject to a critical review the financial policies evolved by central organisations like the University Grants Commission, Indian Council of Agricultural Research, Indian Council of Social Science Research in order to evaluate the correspondence of these policies with the objectives of promoting high level research and nurturing excellence in their respective areas. I am glad that Dr Azad has chosen to undertake a study of these and similar issues in order to arrive at a satisfactory diagnosis of the situation pertaining to the university system and to make suggestions for modifying the system of finance, wherever necessary.

Spotlight has been sought to be focused in this study on some of the important aspects of the financing of higher education—its dichotomies, distortions as also its strong points. The author has taken care to steer clear of unsubstantiated generalisations. This, in my judgement, is a strong point of this study.

While examining the behaviour of aggregative expenditure on education as also on higher education, the study has identified the following trends:

(a) in spite of a continuous rise in the expenditure on education as also on higher education, it is difficult to vouchsafe the adequacy of the financial inputs to meet the ever-rising needs, which are further complicated by the continuous decline in the real value of money;
(b) the behaviour of agencies responsible for financing of higher education has been inconsistent and somewhat erratic; and
(c) the inter-institutional/inter-disciplinary allocation of resources has been somewhat disparate giving rise to the phenomenon of a few comparatively better provided institutions co-existing with the bulk of those leading a precarious existence.

An important contribution of this study is to explode the myth that higher education has been receiving preferential treatment in the allocation of resources by the federal and the state governments. It has also been brought out that, contrary to common belief, there are no diversions of budgetary resources from elementary education (or even school education) to higher education. An analysis of the budgets allotted to various sectors during the period 1968-69 to 1977-78 has revealed that both elementary and secondary education sectors improved their position during the period under review. If at all there were any diversions, they were from "other educational programmes" comprising direction and inspection, cultural programmes, scholarships, games and sports and they were not towards higher education.

The study also reveals the uncomfortable budgetary position of a sizeable proportion of universities. Thirty eight per cent of the universities had "deficit" budgets during the period under review and had to make do with over-drafts or by keeping certain academic positions vacant, besides bringing about economies in other essential spheres.

The procedures of financing of higher education in the states of Andhra Pradesh, Gujarat, Haryana and Orissa were subjected to a critical examination in relation to certain parameters like their effectiveness or otherwise to regulate admissions; to bring about qualitative improvements and to promote academic innovations. The study has revealed that the policies adopted by these states are, by and large, ineffective at least on tw counts; to encourage academic innovations and to restric student admissions.

While the ineffectiveness of the state policies to encourag academic innovations is a serious matter and needs to be reme died, the problem of restricting university admissions is a double edged weapon. The question is extremely complex and is cap able of arousing considerable popular resentment. The economi cally and socially backward classes, which had no tradition o any education in their families for generations have now starte knocking at the portals of university institutions. For obviou reasons, these categories of students would be the worst sufferer in case a policy of selectivity in admissions is adopted purel on the basis of so called "academic merit".

Independent India inherited a highly inequitous system o higher education which was also highly inefficient and dysfunc tional in relation to developmental process. It would not have been desirable to succumb to either populist or elitist pressures and opt for either equity or efficiency. It may, in fact, be stated that within a long range perspective, equity and efficiency are complementary and not contradictory to each other. If the educational level of a large section of the work force is low, the efficiency level of the work force as a whole is bound to be low. Protective discrimination, as a measure of equity, is therefore simultaneously a measure for higher levels of efficiency in a long term perspective. It is quite possible, however, that in the short run, equity and efficiency may be inversely related in some cases. The trade off, therefore, is not between equity and efficiency but between short and long term assessment of efficiency. Only the myopic and the shortsighted would advocate the sacrifice of long term gains at the altar of immediate growth. Only the fanatic and the doctrinaire would close their eyes to the problems of the present. The social concerns for equity and efficiency can, therefore, be only handled together, each sustaining and sustained by each other.

The study also reveals that the system of state grants suffers from quite a few drawbacks like its inequitous character, non-specificity of rules and regulations, inadequacy of quantum of assistance and lack of elasticity and efficiency. It has also been found that the extent of its operation primarily depends on the xigencies of financial situation obtaining at a particular point f time in the states. It is evident that no system of education in flourish, if it suffers from such basic deformities. The sooner ie system of state financing is streamlined, the better it would e for the health of our university institutions.

Dr Azad also focuses attention on the academic bodies being t up in the states, on the pattern of the University Grants ommission. It has been suggested that an academic organisa-on should be interposed between the state bureaucracy and the niversity institutions so that decisions about the allocation of sources should be arrived at not *solely* on the basis of avail-bility of funds but by a scientific assessment of the academic riorities of the university institutions. It is recognised that the ast experience of certain states in setting up such bodies is not ery encouraging. Yet the experiment is worth trying.

It has also been revealed in this study that the grants from ie central organisations suffer from certain incongruities. The ulk of the UGC grants are for the building up of the physical ifrastructure rather than for improving the quality of human iaterial. Further, most central organisations including the GC are more munificent to universities—within them to entral universities—rather than to colleges, which are responsible r over 80 per cent of university enrolment. While it is diffi-ult to question the priorities evolved by these agencies in regard financing of higher education, the comparative neglect of the llegiate institution would necessarily result in a skewed deve-pment of higher education; an eventuality which no central gency would desire to happen.

The study has brought into sharp focus the operation of the hemes of the central organisations about the financing of search. Some of the important findings are:

(a) the various funding organisations have no in-built mechanism of coordination and collaboration among themselves, with the result that duplication and overlap of research effort cannot be avoided.
(b) the bulk of the funds are concentrated in a few institutions and academics. The vast majority of collegiate institutions are not touched by the research support by these bodies.

It is difficult to deny the validity of these observations a
the pernicious effect of these phenomena on the promotion
research. Could it not be possible for these bodies to work o
a system of mutual consultation and coordination so that dup
cation and overlap could be avoided? Further, could not the
organisations distribute their funds more equitably, so that t
so far neglected segments of higher education could also bene
from the schemes of research sponsored by these organisation
Certainly, it is hard to believe that all wisdom and intellect
concentrated in a few institutions and the vast hinterland
higher education is devoid of this quality.

An important problem which has been highlighted in th
study relates to the rapid increases in the proportionate cont
bution of the union and state governments in the financing
higher education and the corresponding diminution of publ
contribution through fees and private donations. The auth
has examined the fast dwindling share of contributions fro
these sources and has made a particular mention of the unec
nomic and unegalitarian character of student fees. While ruli
out a policy of the across the board escalation in student fee
the author has suggested a system of levying *differential* fees
fees on the cost of service principle for those, who are n
suitable for higher studies (and yet desire to go in for high
education), and the usual fees to those, who are academical
suitable. This scheme would also necessitate a much wider e
pansion of the scheme of scholarships and fellowships, so that n
meritorious student would be deprived of educational opportuni
for want of financial means.

The problems of university financing are multi-dimension
and do not admit of a uni-dimensional approach. Me
augmenting of resources is not enough. It is equally essenti
that the available resources should be subjected to appropria
management techniques. Besides, no government can afford, i
the foreseeable future, to provide unlimited resources for educ
tion and hence adequate planning techniques would need to b
applied at the national, state and institutional levels, so th
the available resources could be utilised optimally.

It would be naive to assume that the policy recommendatio
made in the book would prove to be a panacea for the variega
ed problems of higher education finance. It is, however, hop

that the perusal of this book may enable the authorities—both central and state—to view the complex problems of financing higher education in a correct perspective and may sensitise those interested in higher education to the complexities of financing of education at the tertiary level. It may also contribute to the streamlining of the policies, procedures, and patterns of financing of higher education.

It is with this hope that I commend this book to all those concerned with educational development—the administrators, academics and political leaders—who have a desire to improve the system of higher education in our country.

Director,
National Institute of Educational Planning and Administration, MOONIS RAZA

NEW DELHI

July, 1984

that the perusal of the book may enable the audience—both general and specialist—to view the complex problems of financing higher education in a wider perspective and more sensitively. Those interested in higher education through the complexities of financing education at the tertiary level may also contribute to the understanding of the policies, processes and patterns of financing of higher education.

I have much pleasure in commending this book to all those concerned with educational development—the administrators, academics and political leaders—who have a deep interest in the system of higher education in our country.

Director
National Institute of Educational
Planning and Administration, MOONIS RAZA
NEW DELHI

July, 1984

Acknowledgements

THE author expresses his profound sense of gratitude to Professor Moonis Raza, Director, National Institute of Educational Planning and Administration, who not only agreed to provide institutional support for the conduct of this study but also made available ungrudging help and advice at the various stages of this study. He is also grateful to Shri J. Veera Raghavan, presently Educational Adviser to the Planning Commission, who went out of his way to provide encouragement and help in the carrying out of this investigation.

The author is very much indebted to Professor Rais Ahmed, Vice Chairman, University Grants Commission, for going through the manuscript and offering very useful suggestions.

The author's thanks are also due to the educational authorities of various states, Principals of Colleges, Vice-Chancellors, Registrars and Finance Officers of a number of universities, who not only supplied the requisite information about the procedures and patterns of grants, but also spared time to share their experiences about the working of the system of higher educational finance in their respective areas/institutions. The author is also grateful to the concerned officers of the central organizations like the Planning Commission, Ministry of Education, UGC, ICAR, ICHR, ICSSR, who, besides providing information about the policies and programmes of their organisations, were good enough to discuss the various aspects of the financing of higher education. But for their willing cooperation and unstinted assistance, the study would not have seen the light of day.

The author is also appreciative of the very capable assistance given by Dr. (Miss) Bibha Rani, in the compilation of data pertaining to universities and colleges in various states.

The author's thanks are also due to Mrs. Suhasini Ramaswamy, the energetic editor of Concept Publishing Company, for going through the manuscript and offering editorial suggestions.

Last, but not the least, the author is beholden to his wife, Mrs. Dayawati Azad, whose selfless devotion, unlimited forbearance and untiring assistance were a great asset in the timely completion of this study.

J. L. AZAD

Contents

List of Tables

Introduction

THE system of education in general and higher education in particular has been subjected to sharp criticism for its failure to provide education relevant to the needs and aspiration of the teeming millions of this country. Its *apparent* incapacity to promote socio-economic regeneration of the country has evoked cynicism even among its most ardent supporters.[1] It has been pointed out that the system of higher education has developed an inbuilt process of metabolic degeneration in that about half of the students entering the portals of university institutions are thrown by the wayside resulting in a huge loss of financial and human resources. The phenomenon of escalating unemployment and underemployment of university educated persons has further aggravated the situation.

All these factors have led to serious questioning about the effectiveness of higher education to fulfil its twin objectives of extending the frontiers of knowledge and accelerating the process of socio-economic development. The initial euphoria caused by the studies relating to the "production function" of education particularly of higher education—is gradually giving place to the feeling that the promotional role of higher education for economic development has been somewhat exaggerated. It is argued that education, by any reckoning, is one of the factors which influence the productivity of labour. There are other equally, if not more, important factors like health, nutrition, housing and so on which go a long way in influencing the quality of labour force and hence its productivity.

We do not propose to enter into the controversy about the economic value of education and higher education. We do believe that education exercises a decisive influence on the process of socio-economic development although it may be difficult to quantify precisely the extent of its contribution. We also believe that by sharpening the student's intellectual capabilities and giving him access to, and competence in skills, sophisticated and otherwise, higher education does accelerate the process of socio-economic growth and development. While saying this, we do not minimise the contribution of other factors like health, sanitation, nutrition and so on.

The unseemly part of this controversy is that in the welter of denigration of higher education, the factors limiting the effectiveness of the system of higher education have been, by and large, disregarded. It is conveniently forgotten that, particularly after the attainment of political emancipation, the system of higher education has been subjected to considerable strain on account of a ceaseless stream of young aspirants for higher education, not all of whom are suitable for entering its portals. The craze for proliferating institutions of higher education, regardless of their academic justifications, has also led to the gradual erosion of academic standards. Further, the apparent inability or the unwillingness, of the government to provide a sound financial base to the institutions of higher education has also been a serious limiting factor. The situation has been aggravated further by the almost drying up of contribution from private philanthropy. If, in the process, institutions of varying types, dimensions and quality come into being, the reasons would not be far to seek.

The situation has been complicated by the widely varying, and sometimes confusing, procedures and policies adopted by the central and the state governments for providing financial support to institutions of higher education, the largest proporttion of which are under private managements. There is no clear-cut demarcation between the central and the state governments in regard to provision of assistance either in terms of the institutions or in respect of the schemes of development. The government support is often inconsistent and erratic and appears to be based on a policy of ad-hocism, born largely out of the exigencies of the financial situation obtaining at a given point of time in different states.

An analysis of the subsidies from the federal government

reveals the absence of a well defined policy of institutional development. The federal government, though responsible for coordination and determination of standards of the institutions of higher education, has a centrifugal configuration. The assistance to the institutions of higher education comes from a variety of sources, having little coordination among themselves. The University Grants Commission, which is the main instrument of the federal government to implement its responsibility of coordination and determination of standards of higher education and research has an extremely limited role; its jurisdiction does not ordinarily extend beyond institutions concerned with education of a non-professional type. There are quite a few other structural and administrative limitations, which thwart the effectiveness of this apex organisation,[2] concerned with providing the much needed financial sustenance for institutions of higher education.

The grant-in-aid rules of some of the state governments are, in some cases, anachronistic in character and are not attuned to the changing requirements of the university institutions. The main thrust of these regulations is on administrative and financial aspects of university institutions rather than on academic improvement. With a few exceptions, they allow little room for innovations and experimentation in university institutions, A number of state governments have failed to pursue a rational and goal-oriented policy of financing of institutions of higher education. In quite a few states, the rules discourage rather than promote mobilization of resources, so needed for the integrated development of institutions of higher education.

The procedures and policies of state assistance to institutions of higher education do not always encourage planned institutional development.[3] By and large, they seem to be based on a policy of "drift" under which an enterprising private body, not necessarily motivated by academic considerations, can set up an institution of higher education and lay claim for government subsidy. In a large number of states, the institutions have to wait for a specified period before being eligible for government assistance. This gives rise to a number of complications. In the absence of government assistance, the institutions are hardly in a position to provide educational facilities of the requisite standard with the result that an indifferent type of education is given to the students. The absence of a proper check at the time of the initial setting up of the institution also results in private bodies with predominantly extra educational motives being encouraged to set up institutions, which, at a later stage, the state governments are incapable of regulating for fear of antagonising public opinion.

The confusion is accentuated because of lack of specificity in the university regulations about the affiliation of institutions. A number of university acts vaguely define the conditions which the institutions must fulfil before they can be granted affiliation. For example, a large number of university acts either do not make any specification about the financial position of the new institutions or have contented themselves with a vague suggestion that the financial resources should be such as to enable "due provision for its continued maintenance and efficient working." In the case of buildings and equipment, which are important components of physical facilities, most of the university regulations insist upon their "suitability" and "adequacy". About staff, the university acts only insist on their "adequacy" for teaching functions. Similarly the quantum of finances that the private bodies must invest at the initial establishment of the institution has been left somewhat vague. Even when a specific provision is mentioned, it is not always insisted upon. The result of the imprecise definition of the conditions of affiliation is that there is room for manoeuvrability and decisions tend to be taken on other than academic considerations.

There is a plethora of organisations concerned with the task of promoting and financing research in the university and non-university institutions. Besides, a number of federal and state government departments provide financial assistance for research programmes in specific fields. There is, however, no in-built mechanism of mutual consultations and cooperation. In such a situation overlap and duplication of efforts, resulting in wastage of scarce physical, financial and human resources cannot be avoided. Further, there is inadequate machinery for monitoring and feedback in respect of researches undertaken by individual researchers or institutions. Quite a few voluminous reports, prepared at hugh cost to the exchequer, adorn the forgotten shelves of the universities and sponsoring organisations.

The preceding paragraphs list some of the major problems of administration and finance confronting university institutions in India. Quite a few of these problems have been examined by the commissions and committees appointed from time to time by the central and the state governments and the University Grants Commission. Of late, the Indian Council of Social Science Research and some universities have also encouraged studies of the various aspects of university education. Not much attention has, however, been given to the problems of financing of education, with particular reference to the policies and procedures of government support for higher education and research. This study is a modest attempt to fill this gap by probing the system of financing of institutions of higher education evolved by the federal and the state governments and their specialised agencies.

The specific objectives of the study are:

1. To analyse the patterns, procedures and policies of financing of institutions of higher education as well as research adopted by the federal and the state governments and specialised agencies set up by the government.
2. To examine certain basic policy issues pertaining to government support with particular reference to some current practices introduced by the state governments like salary grants, incentive grants, etc.
3. To make suggestions, wherever necessary, for streamlining the policies and procedures of financing institutions of higher education adopted by government.

Since the bulk of the private colleges are concerned with humanities, social sciences, physical sciences, education, engineering and technology, and so on, the study has been delimited to the institutions catering to these disciplines. In the case of research, the procedures and policies of funding adopted by the specialised agencies for agriculture and medicine etc. have also been examined.

A word about the data for this study. The information about the overall finances of university institutions was collected from a variety of sources like the Planning Commission, the Ministry of Education, University Grants Commission and the state governments. The data relating to the patterns and procedures of state grants was collected from the directorates of education of the state governments and union territories. Similar information was obtained from the concerned departments of the federal government and funding agencies like the University Grants Commission, Indian Council of Agricultural Research and Indian Council of Medical Research, etc. The information collected from the state governments was rechecked with the concerned departments of states.

In order to elicit the views of those concerned with the financing of higher education, three sets of questionnaires, one data schedule and one interview schedule were drawn up. One questionnaire was meant to solicit the experiences, views of the respondents about the working of the government procedures and practices of support for higher education. The questionnaire was mailed to 356 principals of colleges representing a cross-section of institutions of higher education. Complete responses were received from 144 institutions.

The second questionnaire was mailed to the vice-chancellors of 89 universities and 54 experts consisting of professors of economics and education and those concerned with the administration and financing of higher education. Responses were received from 25 vice-chancellors and 11 experts.

In order to study the problems of higher education finance in depth, it was decided to undertake a micro-level investigation in 4 states—one in each region of the country. These states were Andhra Pradesh in the south, Orissa in the east, Haryana in the north and Gujarat in the west. As a first step, the system of grant-in-aid for colleges and universities in these states was studied. The reports of special committee(s) appointed by these states to consider the problems of higher education finance were also gone through. Based on this study, detailed questionnaire and data-schedule relating to problems of higher education finance were drawn up, and sent to about 20 per cent of the total number of colleges of different types (except agricultural and medical colleges) and 2 universities in each of the above states. The number of institutions responding in each state (except Orissa, from where no response from colleges was received) is as follows:

Number of Institutions Responding

State	Government	Private	Total	Universities
Andhra Pradesh	11	25	36	1
Gujarat	9	20	29	–
Haryana	7	12	19	1
Orissa	–	–	–	–
Total	27	57	84	2

Out of the above mentioned colleges, 9 colleges belonged to the professional category that is, engineering and technolgy, teacher training and law. The universities which responded were of teaching cum affiliating type.

Personal discussions were also organised with the concerned authorities of the U.G.C., I.C.A.R., I.C.H.R., and other funding agencies about the working of the grant-in-aid schemes sponsored by them and the problems that they were facing in regard to the implementation of their programmes. The problems peculiar to the 4 states were also discussed with the principals of colleges, education secretaries, directors of higher education and technical education and other concerned officers in the respective states.

The author was confronted with problems galore while carrying out this study—the collection of latest data about the financing of higher education being the most intractable. While the information about development outlays was available from the plan documents as also the records of the Planning Commission, Ministry of Education and state governments, the data about university-wise expenditure was simply not available for the recent years. Further, the break-up of what is called "indirect" expenditure on higher education (i.e., on buildings, equipment and so on) was also not available.

Eliciting the views of the high and mighty in the academic world through a mailed questionnaire stands out as the most frustrating experience in the author's life. Some of the most urbane, mild mannered intellectuals, who were approached to give their views, chose to observe a sphinx-like silence—and no coaxing and cajoling would work! They were prepared to discuss—at length—but to reduce their ideas to writing was a tall order, which they did not relish. So the author had to adopt the technique of personal interviews in a number of such cases.

The collection of information about the policies and procedures of federal and state governments presented a different kind of problem. Here the question was to keep track of the latest changes that have, of late, been occurring. This is more so in the case of the procedures and patterns of grants adopted by the state governments. It is possible that in spite of the best efforts to collect the most up-to-date information, some latest changes might have escaped the attention of the author.

In spite of limitations of data and other problems, it is hoped that the analysis presented in this book will be of some help to those concerned with the funding of higher education in this country. The author would feel amply rewarded, if this study evokes some rethinking on the part of the government—federal and states—and results in a revamping of the policies and procedures of support for higher education and research.

The author is not unmindful of the fact that the distortions that the system of higher education has developed are due to a vast array of complex factors. It is also conceded that provision of finances, howsoever adequate, and the revamping of the financial proedures and policies are not sufficient to bring about the much desired changes in university institutions. It is, however, difficult, to deny that rationalisation of the financial policies will go a long way in improving the system of higher education and making it an effective instrument of socio-economic development. It is with this objective that the author has ventured to present this study.

NOTES AND REFERENCES

1. Ironically, the University Grants Commission, which is responsible for the determination and coordination of standards of higher education has come out with a scathing criticism of the system of higher education. The Commission says: "The system of higher

education is now in a state of crisis, due to uncontrolled and unplanned expansion, indequate inputs in terms of money, materials and talents falling standards in a large proportion of institutions, weakening of student motivation, increase of educated unemployment, weakening of discipline and dysfunctioning created by adverse effect of socio-economic problems, a lack of relevance and significance . . , " (UGC: Development of Higher Education in India—A Policy Frame, 1978).

2. For a detailed discussion, see the author's publication: *Financing of Higher Education in India*, (Sterling), 1975.
3. The latest to lament about the "serious lack of planned and need-based development of higher education" is the Committee on Establishment of New Colleges (1979) appointed by the Government of Orissa (See p. 1).

1

UNIVERSITY FINANCES
A Panoramic View

THE SYSTEM of higher education in India does not present a homogeneous, identifiable configuration; it is characterised by heterogeneity and diversity. This is apparent from the large variations in the size, type and quality of institutions, which constitute Indian higher education. At one extreme are the comparatively 'affluent' institutions like the Indian Institutes of Technology, central universities and the specialised institutes in social and physical sciences. At the other end of the scale are the colleges, the academic 'proletariats', mainly catering to education in humanities and social sciences, which are, in terms of the availability of finances, leading a precarious existence. About 50 per cent of such institutions are non-viable, in that they do not fulfil the minimum requirements of enrolment and staff laid down by the University Grants Commission. A study of the financing of higher education in India has, therefore, to reckon with the "vast, unruly assortment of disparate elements"[1] that constitute the university system.

THE AGGREGATIVE ANALYSIS

The analysis of the behaviour of higher education finances reveals the following trends :

(i) A continuous rise in the expenditure on higher education, although in no way approaching a position of adequacy of resources;

(ii) inconsistent and erratic behaviour of agencies responsible for financing higher education.

(iii) disparate character of inter-institutional allocations and resources;

A brief discussion of these trends follows.

Rising expenditures

The expenditures on education and higher education during the post-independence period have marked significant increase. The total expenditure on education increased from Rs. 114 crores per annum in 1951 to about Rs. 5,000 crores in 1983-84. The corresponding increase in higher education was from Rs. 18 crores to Rs. 500 crores. As a proportion of the national income, the increase in the financial allocations for education was from 1.3 per cent to 3.9 per cent for education and from about 0.2 per cent to about 0.6 per cent in the case of higher education.

The developmental expenditure on education also increased significantly during the successive five year plans; from Rs. 153 crores in the first plan, it rose to Rs. 911 crores in the fifth plan (1974-78). For the sixth plan, an outlay of Rs. 2,524 crores has been provided. In terms of proportions to the total plan outlays, however, the education sector has undergone considerable reduction. From 7.6 per cent in the first plan, the proportion of educational expenditure to the total plan outlay was reduced to 3.3 per cent in the fifth plan. In the sixth plan, the proportion has been further reduced to 2.6 per cent. The corresponding decline in the university education has also been quite substantial : from 0.7 per cent in the first plan to 0.3 per cent in the sixth plan.

Inter-sectoral priorities

It has also been noted that during the first five plan periods, the expenditure on higher education (including technical education) has been increasing in proportionate terms to the overall plan expenditure on education; from about 22 per cent in the first plan, it rose to about 34 per cent in the fifth plan. In the sixth plan, however, the outlay for university education has been kept on a low key; it is about 30 per cent of the overall plan outlay on education.

The Table 1.1 illustrates the inter-sectoral priorities in terms of plan outlays during the successive five year plans.

It would appear that there have been substantial shifts in the inter-sectoral expenditures/outlays over the plan periods. In the first plan, foremost priority was given to elementary education, which accounted for more than half of the expenditure on education during that period. This position was, however, not sustained during the subsequent plan periods. In the second to fifth plan, elementary education could muster only about one-third of the plan outlay on education. Secondary education has, however, been able to maintain its position and has been responsible for a little less than one-fifth of the total outlay during the first five plans. The university sector, excluding technical education which was given very low priority in the first plan and accounted for barely 9 per cent of the total outlay, was able to improve its position considerably over the successive five year plans. In the fifth plan, it was responsible for 23 per cent of the plan outlay. In case technical education is also taken into account, the expenditure for post-secondary education would rise from 23 per cent in the first plan to 34 per cent in the fifth plan.

In the sixth plan, a determined effort has been made to provide somewhat larger outlays for elementary education and adult education. In proportionate terms, elementary education and adult education account for about two-fifths of the total plan outlays for education. As a corollary to this, the outlay for university sector has suffered a proportionate reduction. It is, however, difficult to hazard a guess about the extent to which the elementary and adult education sectors would be able to withstand the onslaughts of successive plan revisions, which have been the normal feature of the planning of education in the country.

Myths and realities

At this stage, it is relevant to examine some of the widely held beliefs about the financing of higher education vis-a-vis other sectors of education. Some of these are :

TABLE 1.1: **Expenditures/outlays in the five-year plans**

(*Rs. in crores*)

Sub Head	First Plan	Second Plan	Third Plan	Interrugnum (1966-69)	Fourth Plan	Fifth Plan (1974-78)	Sixth Plan
Elementary Education	85 (56)	95 (35)	201 (34)	75 (23)	239 (30)	292 (32)	905 (36)
Secondary Education	20 (13)	51 (19)	103 (18)	52 (16)	140 (18)	166 (18)	420 (17)
University Education	14 (9)	48 (18)	87 (15)	77 (24)	195 (25)	204 (22)	486 (19)
Adult Education	5 (3)	4 (1)	2 (Neg.)	3 (1)	4.5 (1)	27 (3)	128 (5)
Other Programmes	9 (6)	23 (8)	64 (11)	30 (10)	89.5 (11)	113 (13)	223 (9)
Total General Education	133 (87)	221 (81)	457 (78)	237 (74)	668 (85)	802 (88)	2162 (86)
Art & Culture	*	3 (1)	7 (1)	4 (1)	12 (2)	(*)	84 (3)

Technical Education	20 (13)	49 (18)	125 (21)	81 (25)	106 (13)	109 (12)	278 (11)
Total Education	153 (100)	273 (100)	589 (100)	322 (100)	786 (100)	911 (100)	2524 (100)

(Figures in parantheses indicate percentages)

Source: Planning Commission.

*Included in term 5 (other programme).

Note: The figures denote expenditures from first to fifth plans. In the sixth plan, however, only outlays have been indicated.

(a) Higher education is getting preferential treatment as against other sectors of education. The reason for this is stated to be that the higher education sector is more vocal than other sectors of education. Accessibility to corridors of power is also another causative factor.

(b) even after the budgetary allotments have been made, higher education gets additional resources through transfer of funds from other sectors, particularly elementary education.

A critical examination of the above-mentioned statements follows:

Preferential treatment

In order to examine the question of preferential treatment to higher education, data about sector-wise distribution of overall expenditure under the central and state governments was collected for a twelve year period, that is, 1968-69 to 1980-81.

The Table 1.2 sums up the position :

It would appear that the proportions of expenditure on higher education increased by one percentage point, that is, from 12.2 per cent to 13.2 per cent during the period under review. As against this, the percentage expenditure on elementary education increased by more than 5 percentage points. In the case of school education as a whole, the proportionate increase was from 70.2 per cent to 79.2 per cent, that is, by 9 percentage points. Thus the 'preferential treatment' theory is not sustained by any statistical evidence. A regretable fact that comes to light is that the proportionate increases were effected by drastically reducing the expenditure on 'special education' including adult education and 'other programmes' whiah encompass important programmes like scholarships, equipment, games and sports and cultural programmes and so on.

Diversion of outlays

In order to study the question of diversion of outlays from elementary and secondary education to higher education, the budgeted outlays and actual expenditures for the period 1968-69 to 1977-78 were aggregated. Table 1.3 illustrates the position :

TABLE 1.2: **Sector-wise distribution of total educational expenditure by education departments**

(Revenue Account) (*Rs. in crores*)

Year	Elementary education	Secondary education	Special education including adult education	University and higher education	Technical education	Youth programmes	Others	Total
1968-69	273.84	182.12	16.64	79.21	31.34	0.33	65.66	649.14
	(42.2)	(28.0)	(2.6)	(12.2)	(4.8)	(0.1)	(10.1)	(100.0)
1978-79	1091.23	751.89	39.56	379.61	111.44	39.16	71.54	2484.43
	(44.0)	(30.3)	(1.6)	(15.1)	(4.5)	(1.6)	(2.9)	(100.0)
1980-81	1496.07	996.15	48.34	415.12	90.26	47.77	53.01	3146.72
	(47.5)	(31.7)	(1.5)	(13.2)	(2.9)	(1.5)	(1.7)	(100.0)

Sources: 1. *Trends of Expenditure*, Ministry of Education, 1979, p. 17.
2. *Analysis of Budgeted Expenditure on Education*, Ministry of Education, 1982, p. 161-63.

TABLE 1.3 : Educational expenditures—revenue account (1968-69 to 1977-78)

(Rs. crores)

	Budget	Percentage to total	Actuals	Percentage to total
Elementary education	5470.63	46.1	5910.87	47.8
Secondary education	3627.65	30.5	3968.96	32.1
Special education including adult education	172.96	1.5	142.27	1.1
University and higher education	1205.87	10.1	1339.60	10.8
Technical education	402.57	3.4	391.92	3.2
Sports and youth services	107.23	0.9	116.87	1.0
Other educational programmes	882.69	7.5	489.49	4.0
Total	11,869.60	100.0	12,359.98	100.0

Source : *Trends of Expenditure*—1968-69—1978-79, pp. 33-34.

Here also, the same position emerges. Except for special education including adult education, technical education and 'other programmes', the actual expenditures on all other sectors exceeded the budgeted outlays.

The conclusion that may be drawn is that there is no substance in the common beliefs mentioned above. The higher education sector is as much susceptible to curtailment of outlays as any other sector of education. It is, however, unfortunate that the state governments, harassed by the rising enrolments, are allocating larger outlays for quantitative expansion, that is, opening of schools and colleges, appointing staff and providing other services rather than spending on scholarships, direction and inspection, cultural programmes and so on, which are no less important for educational development.

Inter-state comparisons

A comparative study of the states 'effort' and 'capacity' to spend on education

The 'effort' in this context means the per capita expenditure on education as also on higher education and the 'capacity' is signified by the per capita net domestic product for different states. The relationship between the per capita net domestic product and the per capita expenditure on education as a whole as also of per capita (direct) expenditure on elementary, secondary and higher education was sought to be measured by computing rank correlations among these variables. The state-wise computations have been given in Appendix I. The following table 1.4 summarises the results :

TABLE 1.4 : **Rank coefficients of correlation between per capita NDP of states and per capita expenditures on education—total education, elementary, secondary and higher education**

	1960-61	1965-66	1970-71	1975-76	1980-81
NDP and total education	0.78	0.63	0.65	0.71	0.56
NDP and elementary education	0.50	0.39	0.42	0.42	0.30
NDP and secondary education	0.63	0.71	0.73	0.82	0.54
NDP and higher education	0.74	0.58	0.46	0.37	0.19

The following may be noted :

1. There has been overall diminution in the coefficients of correlation between the per capita net domestic product and all other sectors of education during 1961-81. It means that, over the years, the net domestic product is fast becoming an irrelevant factor so far as expenditure on education is concerned.
2. In the case of higher education, the relationship has

indicated a consistent decline so much so that the co-efficient of correlation in 1980-81 is extremely insignificant. This clearly shows that, through a deliberate policy, the states have not provided funds for higher education consistent with the quantum of NDP.

Inter-state variations in per capita investment in education

The following table 1.5 summarises the inter-state variations between per capita NDP and the per capita expenditure on education as a whole as well as among the various sectors of education :

TABLE 1.5 : **Coefficients of variation among the per capita NDP and per capita expenditure on education as well as its components.**

Year	Per capita NDP	Per capita expenditure on education	Per capita expenditure on		
			Elementary education	Secondary education	Higher education
1960-61	19.22	30.07	42.69	50.10	48.00
1965-66	29.48	24.40	30.50	37.50	28.52
1970-71	24-62	27.26	46.52	45.97	31.09
1975-76	22.20	33.67	39.00	46.33	34.38
1980-81	32.31	34.48	38.93	47.33	30.97

The following may be noted :

(i) No definite trend is discernible in the inter-state variations in the per capita expenditure on education as well as in regard to its break-up among different sectors of education. The data reveals wide fluctuations in the individual years.

(ii) taken as a whole, the inter-state variations in the case of per capita NDP and the per capita expenditure on education have increased.

(iii) in the case of secondary and higher education, there has been a decline in the extent of inter-state variations. In case, however, 1960-61 is excluded, the extent of variations appears to have substantially increased in all the sectors.

The analyses made above reveals that, considered from an all-India point of view, the extent of relationship between the NDP and the expenditure on education has tended to decline. The decline is much more pronounced in the case of higher education. This means that the states have not been providing for outlays in relation to their 'capacity' as revealed by the per capita net domestic product.

The above study of the behaviour of the individual states also brings out an extremely erratic formulation of sectoral inputs in the different states. The absence of a definite trend in the expenditure patterns reveals a policy of ad-hocism in the allocation of resources rather than a definite well considered policy of financing of educational programmes consistent with the broad policies enunciated by the central and the state governments from time to time.

Disquieting features

In spite of the continuous increase in expenditure over the five year plans, the financing of higher education has shown a few disquieting trends. The following may be particularly mentioned :

Financial inadequacy

The overall financial position of the universities and colleges, barring a few exceptions, is far from satisfactory. The inadequacy of finances available to the university institutions does not need a very complicated statistical analysis. The general shortage of educational facilities available with the university institutions is an eloquent testimony to the inadequacy of the finances with these institutions. The various committees and commissions, which examined this problem, have also dwelt at length on this issue.[2] Recently, the Review Committee of the UGC, which examined this question, alluded to the inadequacy of grants from the state governments to the universities and colleges.[3]

In order to assess the financial position of the universities from the point of view of its adequacy, data in respect of 29 universities for 8 years between 1966-67 to 1974-75 was analysed. Cumulative frequencies were computed in respect of those universities having 'surplus', 'deficit' or 'balanced' budgets over the years under study. It was revealed that 38 per cent of th universities had deficit budgets. It means that almost two ou of every five universities were facing the problem of shortag of resources in that expenditures exceeded their incomes.

Comparative neglect of colleges for general education

The Table 1.6 indicates percentage expenditure on differen constituents of education during the period 1960-61 t 1975-76 :

TABLE 1.6 : **Expenditure on different institutions**[4]

(*Figures in percentages*)

Head of expenditure	1960-61	1970-71	1975-76
(a) Indirect expenditure	25.2	14.0	14.8
(b) Direct expenditure :			
(i) Universities	4.1	6.3	6.4
(ii) Boards of secondary education	0.7	1.0	1.0
(iii) Research institutions	0.8	0.2	0.2
(iv) Colleges for general education	6.1	8.4	8.3
(v) Colleges for professional education	4.6	8.1	7.2
(vi) Colleges for special education	0.3	0.2	0.1
(vii) School education (elementary and secondary education)	58.2	61.8	62.0
Total	100.0	100.0	100.0

The following points may be noted :

(i) There has been decline in the proportionate expenditur on indirect items. This signifies that less priority ha been accorded to buildings, equipment and other infra structure of educational institutions.

(ii) higher priority has been given to universities notwith standing the fact that they are responsible for only

17 per cent of student enrolment. The colleges of general education have scraped through with a modest increase in the proportionate expenditure. This is in spite of the fact that these colleges are responsible for 83 per cent of the enrolment at the undergraduate stage, 45 per cent at the post-graduate stage and 15 per cent at the research stage.

(iii) the research institutions have also suffered a steep diminution in the proportionate expenditure devoted to them. From 0.8 per cent of the total expenditure in 1960-61, these institutions accounted for only 0.2 per cent of the expenditure in 1975-76.

The disparate treatment meted out to the colleges of general education is also borne out by the analysis of grants paid by the UGC for universities and colleges. For this purpose, the total grants paid by the UGC to universities and colleges during the period 1975-76 to 1981-82 were aggregated. The total grants paid by the UGC during the period under review accounted for Rs. 225.08 crores for universities and Rs. 50.48 crores for colleges. This works out to Rs. 643 per student in the universities and Rs. 29 per student in the case of colleges. This means that the per student grants for the universities were 22 times more than those given to colleges, while the enrolment catered to by the universities was almost one fifth of the enrolment in colleges :

Impact of inflationary pressures

In order to assess the impact of runaway inflation, that the Indian economy has been subjected to for quite some time, on the finances of institutions of higher education, the following procedure was adopted:

(i) The overall direct expenditure on education as well as the expenditure on higher education was broken down into two broad categories :
   (a) teacher costs including the costs on the administrative staff; and
   (b) non-teacher costs representing the expenditure on equipment, buildings and so on.

(ii) the teacher costs were deflated by applying the consume price indices and the non-teacher costs were subjected t whole-sale price indices.[5]

The position emerging from this computation is summarise in Table 1.7.

TABLE 1.7 : Per student cost on education at current and constant prices (1950-51 to 1980-81)

(Figures in rupees) (1960-61=100)

Year	Total expenditure on education		Total direct expenditure on higher education	
	Current prices	Constant prices	Current prices	Constant prices
1950-51	44.78	51.94	407.98	477.34
1955-56	55.95	75.55	426.79	568.75
1960-61	71.80	71.80	557.34	557.34
196 -56	88.16	66.82	646.68	489.99
1970-71	116.63	64.26	886.00	502.44
1975-76	188.12	59.92	1012.67	350.92
1980-81 (Budget)	282.59	76.58	1139.02	357.10

It would be found that although, at current prices, the per student cost has increased considerably, when allowance is made of the inflationary pressures, the increase is either modest or there is positive diminution. For example, in the case of education as a whole, there has been marginal increase in the per student cost during the period 1951-81. In case, however, the period beyond 1956 is taken, the increase in the cost is hardly significant. In the case of higher education, the situation is quite alarming in that besides very steep decline in the per student expenditure, it is difficult to identify any consistent trend in the expenditure pattern during the years under study.

Inconsistent growth

In order to find out the extent of consistency in the growth of per student expenditure on education as a whole and also on higher education, the average annual growth rates of per student expenditure as also of the enrolment for different quinquennia were worked out. Table 1.8 sums us the position :

TABLE 1.8 : **Average annual growth rates**

(Figure in percentages)

Year	Education		Higher education	
	Expenditure	Enrolment	Expenditure	Enrolment
1951-56	5.0	5.5	1.0	19.3
1956-61	5.6	8.3	6.1	10.8
1961-66	4.6	11.4	3.2	10.2
1966-71	6.5	3.3	7.4	9.9
1971-76	12.6	3.1	2.8	11.4
1976-81	14.5	3.0	18.4	14.2

It would be noted that in the case of education as a whole as well as higher education, there is very little relationship between the growth rates in enrolment and expenditure over the years. These two variables seem to be growing independently of each other. Further, in the case of higher education (except for the last quinquennium), the growth rates of enrolment have far outstripped the corresponding growth rates of expenditure.

Rising expenditure on staff salaries

It has already been pointed out that, in proportionate terms, the expenditure on items like buildings, equipment and so on has been on the decline. It has also been noted that due to successive revisions of salary scales of teachers, the proportionate expenditure on staff salaries has been increasing. Table 1.9 explains the position.

It would be noted there has been substantial decline in the proportionate expenditure on other items in all sectors of education. While in 1950-51, expenditures on staff salaries and other items were almost equally balanced in the case of overall education, in 1980-81 the expenditure on other items was a little more than one-sixth of the total expenditure. While the proportion of expenditure on other items has declined in all sectors, the diminution in higher education has been quite

TABLE 1.9 : Proportionate expenditure on staff salaries and other items in education and higher education

(Figures in percentages)

Year	All education		Higher education	
	Staff salaries	Other items	Staff salaries	Other items
1950-51	52.0	48.0	44.4	55.6
1955-56	51.6	48.4	47.2	52.8
1960-61	46.1	53.9	40.9	59.1
1965-66	65.3	34.7	64.5	35.5
1970-71	72.6	27.4	66.5	33.5
1975-76	81.4	18.6	73.2	26.8
1980-81	85.0*	15.0	73.3**	26.2

*Estimated.

**Relates to 84 private colleges in Andhra Pradesh, Gujarat and Haryana.

sizeable : from a little more than one half of the total direct expenditure in 1950-51, it declined to almost one fourth of the expenditure in 1980-81.

An inference that could be drawn from this analysis is that, over the years, ihe state governments have been, through compulsions of circumstances, providing increasingly higher outlays for teachers' salaries and other staff salaries, to the comparative neglect of the educational infrastructure : building, equipment, library, and so on. Much of it could be accounted for by the successive revisions of the staff salaries made by the state governments. While one would not grudge the improvement in the financial position of the teachers and other supporting staff, the neglect of the physical inputs—no less important in the educational system—can hardly be taken with equanimity.

SOURCES OF FINANCE

The disquieting features identified in the aggregative analysis of financing of higher education made above necessitate a closer look at the procedures and policies of financing of higher education adopted by the central and the state governments and their specialised agencies. While this analysis would be attempted in the subsequent chapters, it appears appropriate to examine briefly the major trends in the behaviour of important sources of university finances.

The statement in the Appendix II indicates the contribution made by important sources to 84 private general education colleges located in the states of Andhra Pradesh, Gujarat and Haryana. It would be seen that except Haryana, the state governments have emerged as the major contributory factor to the financing of higher education. Further, except for Andhra Pradesh, there has been perceptible decline the proportionate contribution from fees and endowments. This phenomenon of diminishing private contributions including tuition fees merits a somewhat extended discussion.

Tuition fees

As already stated, the proportionate contribution from fees has been on the decline because the fee structure has remained almost static in spite of a steep rise in the costs of the educational apparatus. The question as to what extent the fees should be linked with the rising costs of education opens up the flood-gates of controversy and, therefore, needs to be examined in depth. This has been attempted in a subsequent chapter. At this stage, it is sufficient to say that higher education, unlike elementary education, is not the constitutional prerogative of every student, who chooses to enter the portals of the universities. The fee-structure should, therefore, be determined keeping in view, to a very great extent, the economic value of university education. This would also necessitate the provision of suitable incentives for financially weaker sections of the society.

Private benefactions

The relative contribution from private philanthropy has been consistently on the decline. Various reasons have been attributed to the decline in private munificence which include the extinction of the princely order, the abolition of the zamindari system and the decline of landed aristocracy as also the apparent incapacity of the middle classes to invest in education due to spiralling inflation and so on. The restricted nature of tax remissions for donations to educational institutions also exercises a curbing influence on the enthusiasm of the business houses to contribute to education. Further, the rising unemployment among the university educated persons seems to have engendered the feeling about the futility of investing in education at that stage and thus giving an impetus to the mushrooming of institutions, which at best produce unemployed, if not unemployable, graduates. The question of mobilising private resources also merits a more detailed examination, which has been attempted in a subsequent chapter.

Efficiency of the system

Before concluding this discussion, it may be pertinent to say a word about the efficiency of the system of higher education. For the purpose of our discussion, the following variables constitute the dimensions of efficiency :

(a) the wastage and stagnation at the university stage; and
(b) the utilisation of the end product.

(a) So far as the apparent wastage at the university stage is concerned, the position is far from satisfactory. A number of studies have revealed the huge wastage that occurs in universities and colleges in terms of failures in various examinations and the sub-standard quality of those who are successful. It has been reckoned that in humanities and social sciences, about 50 per cent of the students fail to qualify at the undergraduate stage. Out of those, who pass, about three fourths are placed in the lowest grade. Thus about 7 out of 8 students fail to attain a reasonable level of achievement.

(b) The ever increasing unemployment among the university graduates and post-graduates is another positive indicator of the malaise that has afflicted the educational system. The alarming rise in the ranks of the educated unemployed[6] testifies to the existence of some basic inadequacy in the system of higher education as also absorptive capacity of the economy.

The above indicators need not lead one to conclude that the university system is inefficient and uneconomic. This would be an unwarranted condemnation of the system that has produced a large body of intellectuals, scientists and other professionally trained personnel. The point that needs to be stressed is that particularly in the Indian conditions, perennially afflicted by an economy of scarcity, it is inadvisable to permit such colossal wastage of human and material resources that is appening in the educational system in general and in the niversity institutions in particular. There is, therefore, need or a fundamental restructuring of the university system so as avoid the wastage that occurs in our universities and olleges.

o conclude

may be stated that in spite of relatively larger outlays being laced at the disposal of the university system, the behaviour f higher education finance has been erratic and inconsistent. urther, the apparent huge investment in higher education has een substantially eroded by the spiralling inflation in the conomy. The inter-sectoral priorities have not always been uitably worked out. The system is subjected to considerable astage of human and material resources.

It may be too harsh an indictment of the system of higher lucation to describe it as "a massive invalid unable to respond any simple treatment.[7]" The fact, however, remains that e system has developed serious malfunctioning in certain spects and would need sustained treatment of a radical nature order to restore it to a state of near normalcy. Providing e requisite finances for its development is one part of this ercise. An equally important requirement is that the financial olicies and procedures pertaining to higher education should streamlined in order to enable them to accelerate the process rejuvenation of the system of higher education.

The discussion that follows is an attempt in that direction.

NOTES AND REFERENCES

. Chester E. Finn Jr., *Scholars, Dollars and Bureaucrats*, The Brookings Institutions, Washington, 1978, p. 170.

. The University Economy Committee appointed by the Government of Maharashtra (1975) suggested a liberalised pattern of assistance to the universities in Maharashtra. In spite of this, "the universities have again accumulated heavy overdrafts, which they are not in a position to wipe out. They have also incurred large number of outstanding commitments". (Government of Maharashtra Resolution No. USG=1180/174980 (5555/UNI-I dated 4th April, 1981).

3. See Report of the Review Committee on the U.G.C., New Delhi 1977, pp. 58 and 59.
4. 'Indirect' expenditure indicates items like buildings, furniture direction and administration etc., which cannot be apportione separately.
5. Working Class Consumer Price Index for the year 1950-51, 1955-56 and 1960-61, and urban non-manual employees consumer pric index for the later years.
6. The incidence of unemployment among the university educate persons has been measured in a number of studies conducted b the Directorate General of Rehabilitation and Employment an the Planning Commission. According to the latest figures avail able, the number of unemployed university graduates is likely t increase from around 10 million in 1980 to 13.5 million by 1985. (Sixth Five Year Plan, p. 220).
7. Eric Ashby, *Universities : British, Indian, African*, London, Weiden field and Nicolson, 1966, p. 139.

2

A HISTORICAL RETROSPECT

HE CONCEPT of education being a function of the State is of ecent origin, both in the Occident and the Orient. In the ast, education in the West was the function of the organised hurch. In India, however, due to her pluralistic socio- eligious base, it was organised through diverse religious rders, which devised varying systems of education suiting heir peculiar needs. The State, however, made financial contribution on a selective basis for the furtherance of education of its subjects.

In this chapter, it is proposed to make a study of the ystems of financing of education in general and higher education in particular in a historical perspective. While some ttempt will be made to bring out the major contours of the inancial policies and procedures under the Brahmanical, the Buddhist and the medieval periods, the main thrust of the study will be to analyse the financial policies evolved by the British rulers of India including those adopted by the East ndia Company, which preceded the emergence of the 'brigh- est jewel' in the British Crown.

THE BRAHMANICIAL PERIOD

The most ancient educational system in India was the Brahmanical system which dates back to the Vedic Age. It was based on close, intimate and personal relationship between the individual teacher and his small circle of disciples. *Gurugraha* (the teacher's abode) as it was termed then, therefore, became the most natural educational institutio Besides, the oral tradition of teaching imparted to th educational system a kind of sublime simplicity, necess tating minimal financial inputs. It was only at the highe education stage, that the *Brahman Samghas*, the Assemblie or Academies, were established for the advanced studen to gather for knowledge, which was mainly through discussio of various concepts and practices.

The *rishis* in ancient India were regarded as custodian of culture and learning. According to Altekar, they wer required to teach all qualified students free of charge. Even poor student could not be refused admission; he had to b taught in return for personal service and in expectation o some lump sum to be paid later, when he had finished hi education and was in a position to collect subscription fo the purpose.[1] Fee system, as it is understood now, wa conspicuous by its absence. The parents of the students wer asked to note that "no object in the universe, howsove precious it may be, can be regarded as an adequate fee fo even that humble teacher, who teaches a single letter o alphabet".[2] The Yajurveda has described the three debts that a student owes—the foremost being the debt to rishi to be repaid by brahmacharya, by which he is to acquire an spread the knowledge he inherits from the *rishis*. In the late Vedic period, however, the *brahmacharin* used to go abou begging for his teacher. This was not as a quid pro quo fo the knowledge attained, but to inculcate among the student a spirit of humility.

The finance required for the up-keep of the *Samghas* wa to be provided by the state and through the munificence o the rich. There are references to the duty of the king to provide for the up-keep of the learned teachers. In Mahabha rata, Bhishma says to King Yudhishtra: "you should pleas those, who are receiving education according to Vedic rule with gifts of dress and so on and by employing servants for the construction of houses for them".[3] According to Kautilya:

> Brahmins shall be provided with forests for religious learning; those learned in the Vedas shall be granted

Brahmadeya lands yielding sufficient produce and exempt from taxes and fines.[4]

The rich also, at times, contributed liberally for the cause of education by founding free boarding houses, construction of buildings and endowing chairs. The underlying idea was that *vidyadan* (endowment for education) was the greatest gift that one could bestow on his compatriots.

THE BUDDHIST PERIOD

The individualistic system of education that flourished during the Vedic period was replaced by the monastic system ordained by Lord Buddha. The difference is significant since it led to the evolution of two distinct systems of education—a small school with an individual teacher under the Vedic system and "a large educational federation, controlled by a collective body of teachers, as was the characteristic of the Buddhist system."[5]

Founding of universities

The monastic system of education, evolved by the adherents of Buddhism, led to the founding of large universities,[6] with thousands of teachers and students congregating at the same place. The Buddhist education system was thus a natural outgrowth of monasticism, with the universities imbibing some of the characteristics of the monasteries. They were seats of religion, culture and learning. The chief sources of such finances of the universities were two-fold : (1) private endowments and (2) government subventions. Gifts to monasteries were regarded by people and princes alike as an act of spiritual merit. Huin Tsang, who visited Nalanda in the seventh century A.D., has recorded that its grounds were the gift to the Buddha by 500 merchants, who bought them up for as many as 'ten koti of gold coins'.[7] He mentions 'six monasteries as having been built by as many kings, and these constituted the Nalanda establishment in his time.[8] It has also been recorded that "the king of the country remitted the revenue of about 100 villages for the endowment of the convent.[9] No fees were levied for receiving benefits of residence and learning.

THE MEDIEVAL PERIOD

The early Muslim invaders were more interested in conquest and consolidation of their empire than providing for the educational needs of the conquered subjects. After, however, the Muslim rule was somewhat firmly established in parts of India, they turned their attention to education and started setting up educational institutions. It is said that Sultan Iltimush founded one Madrassa at Delhi and another at Multan. Under the Mughal Kings, particularly under Akbar, a number of Madrassas and public libraries were established. Besides the rulers, "there is evidence that the patronage and encouragement of learning, and the foundation of colleges and schools were also undertaken by many of the nobility and gentry . . ."[10] Any organised system of public financing of education or higher education was, however, non-existent.

THE BRITISH PERIOD

Educational finance during the British rule in India may be regarded as an extension of the educational policies which the British government in India adopted from time to time. Educational finance during the British rule could, therefore, be conveniently examined according to four distinct periods or stages of educational policy developments. These four periods cover the history of British educational policy in India from 1600* to 1812 (period I), 1813 to 1901 (period II), 1901 to 1921 (period III) and 1921 to 1947 (period IV).

Period I : (1600 to 1812)

Educational policy during this period (1600-1812) may be said to have been characterised by general apathy towards educational development. The East India Company did not,

*The East India Company was given a Royal Charter on 31st December, 1600. It started as a trading concern but, by a policy of intrigues and conquests, became the ruling power in India.

in the initial stages, show any interest in Indian education partly because it followed in this respect the British practice, and partly because of the organisational and financial limitations.[11] The first attempts by the Company at educating the 'natives' in India were primarily directed towards proselytisation.[12] However, such efforts were feeble, and the Company was reluctant to invest in the education of the Indians. This may be demonstrated by the fact that when Warren Hastings founded the Calcutta Madrassa[13] in 1782, the cost was at first privately defrayed by the Governor-General himself out of an endowment made by his friend and former tutor, Raja Nobikissen. After two years, he was reimbursed by the Company, and the institution was handed over to the government. This was followed by the creation of Banaras Sanskrit College in 1792 by Johnathan Duncan, the British Resident at Banaras. The college was maintained by the government. In Poona, the commissioner of the Deccan started a college for Hindu learning. Part of the fund established by the Peshwa for the support of pundits was utilised for running it. In the Delhi district, Fraser set up schools for the instruction of children of the zamindars in reading and writing the Pesrian language. It is significant that he himself defrayed its expenses to the extent of Rs. 200 per mensem.

Thus the educational efforts of the East India Company during the period (1600-1812) were of a very limited significance. The Company was constrained to restrict their efforts due to the combination of two factors: (1) limited commercial and political objectives requiring severe restriction on its functioning, and (2) constraints of financial resources. Under the circumstances, early attempts at starting educational institutions and their financing were made by individual officers of the East India Company.

Period II (1813 to 1901)

The first break through in the general apathy of the East India Company was provided by the Charter Act of 1813, which placed an amount of Rs. 1 lakh at the disposal of the British Governor for the education of the natives of India. Section 43 of the Charter Act laid down:

> It shall be lawful for the Governor-General in Council to direct that out of any surplus, which may remain of the rents, revenues and profits arising from the said territorial requisition, after defraying the expenses of the military, civil and commercial establishments and paying the interest of the debt, a sum of not less than one lac of rupees in each year, shall be set apart and applied to the revival and improvement of literature and the encouragement of the learned natives of India and for the introduction and promotion of a knowledge of the sciences among the inhabitants of the British Territories in India...[14].

It would appear that the first major Directive relating to the financing of educational programmes by the Government of India was couched in such an unnecessarily legalistic phraseology and hedged with so many provisos that for about two decades not much was done to implement it. Further, it gave rise to a fierce controversy between what have been called the "anglicists" and the 'orientalists' over the manner of expending the amount earmarked for education in India. Macaulay, a member of the Governor General's Council, through his matchless rhetoric, and an uncanny contempt for the Indian and oriental languages which he described as 'poor and rude', spearheaded a virulent attack against these languages and the literature in Sanskrit and Arabic. This he did in spite of his confession that, he had no knowledge of any of these languages.[15] He claimed that he had "never found one among them (the orientalists) who could deny that a single shelf of a good European Library was worth the whole native literature of India and Arabia".[16]

His conclusion was that the government was not fettered by the Act of Parliament of 1813 or by any pledge expressed or implied and that the government should employ the amount "in teaching what is best worth knowing: that English is better worth knowing than Sanskrit or Arabic".[17]

The government's decision announced in Lord Bentinck's Resolution passed in 1835 favoured the point of view of the 'Anglicists'. It said:

> "the great object of the British Government ought to be

> the promotion of European literature and science among the natives of India; and that all the funds appropriated for the purpose would be best employed on English education alone".[18]

The Resolution promised not to abolish any colleges or schools of a native learning, but declared that no stipends would be given to any student that may hereafter enter at any of these institutions. The printing of the oriental works under the auspices of the government was also to be stopped.

The controversy was, however, not resolved. 70 students from the Government Sanskrit College, Calcutta, sent a pathetic petition to the Government against the stoppage of stipends. The Government relented and Lord Auckland in his Minute dated 24th November, 1839, "guaranteed the maintenance of oriental institutions; declared for English instruction in zila schools and the foundation of central colleges. . . ."[19] The Despatch of 1841 from thc court of Directors approved the principles laid down in Lord Auckland's Minute.

> This Minute came to be regarded as an authoritative pronouncement of the educational policy of the Government and all subsequent reforms and improvements up to 1854 were carried out in accordance with this policy.[20]

The vacillating government policy regarding financing of educational expansion in India is reflected in the substantially varying government expenditures on education during this period in the three Presidencies. Table 2.1 explains the position.

By 1854, it was possible to discern a broad delineation of the Government of India's policy relating to financing of education, particularly higher education. It had two main objectives:

(a) Gradual withdrawal of the government from the educational field, and
(b) Encouragement of private enterprise through a system of grant-in-aid.

TABLE 2.1 : **Growth of expenditure on education in the three presidencies**[21]

Year	Bengal £	Madras £	Bombay £	Total £	Indices of Growth
1813	4,207	480	442	5,129	100
1820	5,807	480	1,401	7,688	149.8
1825	57,122	480	8,961	66,563	1297.5
1830	28,748	2,946	12,636	44,330	846.1

(£=*Rs. 10*)

The Despatch of 1854, which laid the foundation for the starting of three universities on the model of the London University, recognised as "one of our most sacred duties to be the means, as far as in us lies, of conferring upon the natives of India those vast moral and material blessings which flow from the general diffusion of useful knowledge.[22] It, however, admitted that it was impossible for the Government alone to do "all that must be done in order to provide adequate means for the education of the natives of India.[23] Keeping in view "the ready assistance, which may be derived from efforts, which have hitherto received but little encouragement from the State", the Government was led to the "natural conclusion that the most effectual method of providing for the wants of India in this subject will be to combine with the agency of the government the aid, which may be derived from the exertions and the liberality of the educated and wealthy natives of India, and other benevolent persons".[24] The Government in fact looked forward to a time, when "any general system of education entirely provided by the Government may be discontinued with the gradual advance of the system of grant-in-aid and when many of the existing institutions especially those of higher order may be safely closed".[25]

The Despatch suggested a system of grant-in-aid to be based on the entire abstinence from religious instruction in the schools assisted. Aid was to be given to all schools which impart secular education, provided they are under adequate local management and provided their managers consent that "the schools shall be subject to government inspection and agree to any conditions, which may be laid down for the regulation of such grants".[26]

The policy of gradual withdrawal of the government from education communicated in the Despatch of 1854 came in for subdued criticism from the Indian Education Commission, 1882, which recommended that the wisest course would be to consider each case (of withdrawal) on merits.[27] The Commission also reiterated the policy of grant-in-aid to institutions of higher education. The Commission, however, disfavoured the system of giving grants "by reference solely to the results of examinations".[28] Another important recommendation made by the Commission was that for the "stability of these institutions, their grants should be fixed for a term of years, so that their managers may be able to estimate with accuracy their sources of income".[29]

The Commission made important recommendations about encouraging private effort in education. Some of the significant recommendations were:

(i) Consulting the managers of non-government institutions on matters of general educational interest, and admitting their students on equal terms to competitions for certificates, scholarships, and other public distinctions;

(ii) publishing revised rules for grant-in-aid, and any subsequent alterations made in them not merely in the official gazettes but their translation into the vernacular, and publication in the Press;

(iii) keeping the fees in all secondary schools and colleges managed by the department as high as possible, and higher than in the aided institutions of a corresponding class. It was also suggested that the fees in every institution should be as high as is consistent with the spread of education in order that the drain on the limited resources of the State may be lessened and funds set free to meet new demands;

(iv) removing departmental institutions, as the area of private effort gradually expanded; and

(v) making a periodically increasing provision in the

educational budget of each province for the expansion of aided education.[30]

It would be seen that it was during the last quarter of the 19th century that the need for evolving a policy framework relating to financing of Indian education was recognised by the government. The Education Commission (1882) laid down positive guidelines relating to such subjects as grant-in-aid policy, fee policy, the methods of securing cooperation from the non-government organisations for setting up educational institutions and the expansion of aided institutions. It was in pursuance of the Education Commission's recommendations that the system of adjusting the quantum of government grant according to the number of pupils, who passed the various examinations was replaced by "other tests based on considerations such as needs and merits of the institutions and the amount of private funds forthcoming. . ."[31] This heralded the evolution of the present system of government grants for institutions of higher aducation.

Period III (1902-21)

This period was marked by increasing central government interest in higher education. The period also saw the extension of the government assistance to the universities. Lord Curzon, "who brought a fresh and vigorous approach to the problem of universities in India",[32] lamented over the misdirection and waste of effort in education for which he would not hold the Government of India free from blame. He urged that the educational system should have "elasticity, flexibility and variety".[33]

The Indian Universities Commission, 1902, which suggested far-reaching changes in the complexion and character of the universities, did not say much about higher education finances except that the fees "must not be pitched so high as to check the spread of education, and secondly, that they must not be fixed so low as to tempt a poor student of but ordinary ability to follow a university course, which it is not to his real interest to undertake. . .".[34]

The period under reference witnessed a number of policy announcements by the Goverement of India on the subject of education. The Government of India's Resolution of March 11, 1904, reaffirmed the Government's policy of "the progressive devolution of primary, secondary and collegiate education upon private enterprise and the continuous withdrawal of Government from competion therewith"[35] as advocated by the Education Commission of 1882 to be adopted with utmost caution. The Resolution, however, underlined "the extreme importance of the principle that in each branch of education, government should maintain a limited number of institutions, both as models for private enterprise to follow and in order to uphold a high standard of education. . .".[36]

The Government's increasing interest in educational development was reiterated by His Majesty, the King Emperor, in reply to the address of the Calcutta University on the 6th January, 1912, in which he expressed the wish that "there may be spread over the land a network of schools and colleges, from which will go forth loyal and manly and useful citizens able to hold their own in industries and agriculture and all the vocations of life. . . ."[37] In pursuance of this declaration, the Government of India announced the following decisions:[38]

(i) Providing assistance to the local governments by means of large grants from Imperial revenues, as funds became available, to extend comprehensive system of education in several provinces;

(ii) liberalisation of grant-in-aid rules; grants to be based on the general efficiency of the institutions and desert rather than rules of calculation; and

(iii) full encouragement to be given for improved and original methods of teaching.

It was during this period that financial assistance was exended to the universities. Prior to 1904, the Government did not give any grant to any university except the Punjab, which received an annual grant of Rs. 30,000 because it conducted the oriental and law colleges. The universities being merely examining bodies did not, in fact, require any grants. "The fees received from examinations were enough to cover their expenses and to provide for the paid servants of the university".[39] The universities Act of 1904, besides increasing their administrative functions made the universities responsible for the inspection of the colleges as well as undertaking direct teaching functions and hence the need for government assistance was felt very strongly.

The first grants to the universities were sanctioned in 1905 and of the total amount of Rs. 25 lakhs to be given in 5 years at an annual rate of Rs. 5 lakhs, Rs. 11½ lakhs were allotted for the administration of the universities, besides buildings and so on and Rs 13½ lakhs were given to the local governments, for the improvement of colleges. In 1913-14, the government grants were raised to Rs. 17 lakhs for buildings, libraries and so on and Rs. 4.03 lakhs per annum for running expenses. These "more generous" grants were given for "providing these institutions with buildings and libraries, befitting their dignity; initiating system of centralised teaching. . . ."[40] During the next quinquennium, the government grants were raised to Rs. 43 lakhs.

The increasing government grants for the universities and colleges and the expanding institutional base brought home the need for bringing about coordination in the field of higher education. The Calcutta University Commission (1917-19) stressed on the Government of India the need to maintain an organisation, which would keep itself continuously "in touch with what is going on in the various universities, as well as other educational grades in all the provinces".[41] Ironically, soon after this recommendation was made, the administrative system known as 'Dyarchy' was introduced and the Government of India ceased to have any responsibility for educational development in the country.

Period IV (1921-47)

Under the Government of India Act, 1919, an administrative system known as *Dyarchy* was introduced, which distributed the activity of the provincial governments into two parts—*Reserved* departments under the executive councillors, who were responsible to the Governor and the *Transferred* departments under ministers responsible to the provincial legislatures. The financial system under Dyarchy envisaged that the provincial governments would make yearly contributions to the central government. These contributions were to be the first charge on the provincial budgets. In the process, the provincial resources were crippled and the transferred subjects including education suffered. This, along with the economic distress that prevailed in the country as the aftermath of the First World War, led to a financial stringency, "which made the curtailment of the education budgets inevitable and the retrenchment policy, which it had been found necessary to adopt during the previous quinquennium (1917-22), was continued for the first few years of the period under review, and until there were signs of a marked improvement in the economic conditions in the provinces, educational development and expansion continued to be seriously retarded".[42]

Another effect of the 'Dyarchy' was that the control and the supervision exercised by the Government of India over education in the major provinces ceased. This was an arrangement with doubtful gains. It resulted into an undue growth of 'provincial exclusiveness' in educational matters. The Government of India tried to bring about some uniformity by establishing the Central Advisory Board of Education in 1921 only to abolish it in 1923 in a time of financial stress "without even a reference to the provincial governments as to the advisability of its continuance . .".[43]

The control of the popular ministers on education under 'Dyarchy' proved to be ill-starred in regard to educational finance. The Quinquennial Review for 1927-32 reported that "economic distress, far exceeding in magnitude and intensity even that experienced in post-war years, has intervened; expenditure has been cut down in all directions; the pace of expansion has been retarded; political life has been disturbed; communal bitterness has been accentuated".[44]

Due to these difficulties, the pendulum again swung in favour of increasing central interest in education. The Hartog Committee (1929) recommended that "constitutional means should be devised to enable the Imperial Government to come to their (Provincial Governments') aid and that the Government of India should not continue to be divested of all powers to make central grants to provincial governments for mass education . .".[45] Nothing significant was, nowever, done in this regard.

With the introduction of the Provincial autonomy under the Government of India Act, 1935, when the Indian Ministers got greater control over finances, hopes were raised that the position of education would improve. These hopes were, however, soon belied by the intervention of the Second World War that necessitated the diversion of all government resources to the prosecution of War. The political turbulence that ensued in the wake of the Quit India Movement also adversely effected the availability of finances for education. During this period again, suggestions were made for increasing the central interest in education. In this connection particular mention may be made of the Committee on Post-War Educational Development in India under John Sargent, the then Educational Commissioner to the Government of India, which insisted that the financial responsibilities for a national system of education must be divided between the central and the provincial governments . . ."Any reallocation of the financial burden between the centre and the provinces should also have regard to variations in the revenue producing capacity of different areas".[46] The Committee also suggested that "half of the total number of university students should be able to pay for their education at a rate of fee somewhat higher than at present . . .[47]

Another very important recommendation made by the Committee was with regard to the setting up of some authority, which would coordinate university education in the country as a whole. The Committee did not suggest that such a body should be under the control of the government. What the Committee contemplated was an organisation on the pattern of the British University Grants Committee. This body was expected to "exercise a general supervision over the allocation of grants to universities from public funds, with the object of ensuring that the universities are in a position to meet the demands, which are made upon them . . ."[48]

It would be seen that this period was generally characterised by financial and political instability. Further, the Government of India was divested of the responsibility of financing and administration of education as well as higher education. The divorce of the central government from higher education, however, did not prove to be beneficial for educational development and strong voices were raised to end this 'constitutional isolation, on the part of the central government. Before anything tangible could, however, be achieved, the Second World War broke out with all its fury and put the entire administrative and financial arrangements out of gear. The end of the War saw India on the threshold of independence. In the short span of two years that intervened between the cessation of hostilities and the attainment of freedom, politics and not education dominated the Indian scene.

EXPENDITURE ON HIGHER EDUCATION

The changes in the government policies during the British period in regard to financing of education in general and higher education in particular were amply reflected in the behaviour of expenditure under these heads. Up to 1902, there was gradual decline in the proportionate contribution by government to educational expenditure : from 56 per cent of the total expenditure in 1881-82, the government contribution was reduced to 44 per cent in 1902. In the case of colleges, the government contribution was reduced from about 57 per cent to about 50 per cent. The universities being purely examining bodies were almost totally dependent upon fees—the government contribution being less than 2 per cent of the expenditure. The following Table 2.2 illustrates the position :

TABLE 2.2 : **Sourcewise expenditure on collegiate institutions—1896-97**

(Rupees in '000)

Head of charge	Provincial revenue	Local fund/ municipal fund	Fees	Other sources	Total
Arts colleges	16.33	43	9,75	6,19	32,70
	(49.9)	(1.4)	(29.9)	(18.8)	(100.0)
Universities	12	1	6,16	42	6,71
	(1.7)	(0.2)	(91.8)	(6.3)	(100.0)
Total education	95,23	72,43	106,11	78,68	3,52,45
	(27.0)	(20.5)	(30.1)	(22.4)	(100.0)

Note : Figures in parantheses indicate percentages

Source : J.S. Cotton, *Progress of Education in India:* 1892-93 to 1896-97 —Third Quinquennial Review; (London, H.M.S.O., 1898) p. 31,

The dwindling government interest in collegiate education led to a diminution in the average annual cost per student in arts colleges during 1886-87 to 1896-97. The following Table 2.3 sums up the position :

TABLE 2.3 : **Average annual cost per student in arts colleges (English)**

Colleges by management	1886-87	1896-97
	(Rs.)	(Rs.)
Departmental	322	269
Municipal	121	147
Native states	406	273
Aided	186	159
Unaided	102	56
Average	199	160

Source : J.S. Cotton, *Progress of Education in India* : 1892-93 to 1896-97—Third Quinquennial Review, p. 98.

The period preceding the introduction of 'Dyarchy' was marked by the First World War and the political turmoil caused by the intensification of the Non-Cooperation Movement which, according to Richey, "succeeded in crippling some schools beyond hope of recovery, in disorganising the work of others for six months or a year and in ruining the careers of many promising scholars. . .".[49] The transfer of education "took place at a time not only of considerable financial stress but also of disturbance in the educational world . . .".[50] By the close of 1922, however, the period of trials and tribulations had passed and, as stated earlier, increasing subventions were made to university institutions during this period. The Table 2.4 indicates the position.

It would be seen that as compared to 1896-97, the universities started receiving much larger sums from the government revenues in 1921-22. Most of the increase in expenditure on universities, was, however, on account of the opening of the Dacca University in Bengal and on account of the capital and other expenditure on the new universities of Lucknow, Banaras and Aligarh. In the case of colleges, the government contribution declined in 1921-22 as compared to 1896-97 but the contribution from fees increased. There was some increase in the contribution from private sources.

TABLE 2.4 : **Sourcewise finances for higher education—1921-22**

(Rupees in '000)

Institutions	Govt. fund	Board fund	Fees	Others	Total expenditure
Universities	22,28	(Negligible)	25,09	28,68	76.05
	(29.3)	(—)	(33.0)	(37.7)	(100.0)
Arts colleges	49,27	47	37,80	22,89	1,10,43
	(44.6)	(0.4)	(34.3)	(20.7)	(100.0)
Total education	902,30	2,47,31	3,80,09	3,07,83	18,37,53
	(49.1)	(13.4)	(20.7)	(16.8)	(100.0)

Note : Figures in parantheses indicate percentages.

Source : *Progress of Education in India*, 1917-22—Eighth Quinquennial Review; Vol. I, (Calcutta, Govt. Printing, India), 1932.
(a) Education p. 15
(b) Universities p. 73
(c) Arts Colleges p. 74

On the eve of Independence, which was preceded by the World War II and the political upheavel caused by the mass upsurge to shake off the yoke of foreign subjugation, the government contribution to collegiate institutions including that of the local bodies stood at about 40 per cent of the total direct expenditure against about 60 per cent for education as a whole. The fees provided the major contribution to the finances of the collegiate institutions—meeting about 45 per cent of the total direct expenditure. The contribution from 'other sources' had declined considerably. Table 2.5 sums up the position of sourcewise contribution to university finances in 1946-47 which heralded the dawn of independence in India,

Summing up

The system of financing of education particularly higher education in the pre-Independence period was subjected to strange vicissitudes of time. It took the East India Company more than a century to officially recognise their responsibility for the education of the vast masses of the people, over whose

TABLE 2.5 : Sourcewise expenditure on institutions of higher education—1946-47.

(*Rupees in '000*)

Institutions	Govern-ment	Local bodies	Fees	Other sources	Total
Direct					
Universities	68,69	—	86,26	37,74	1,92,69
	(35.6)		(44.8)	(19.6)	(100.0)
Colleges	2,82,16	3,59	3,22,35	99,20	7,07,30
	(39.9)	(0.5)	(45.6)	(14.0)	(100.0)
Total (direct & indirect expnd. on education)	20,45,27	6,52,49	11,57,12	6,62,00	45,16,88
	(45.3)	(14.4)	(25.6)	(14.7)	(100.0)

Note : Figures in parantheses indicate percentages.

Source : *General Education Tables for India*—1946-47; Ministry of Education (Bureau of Education, India, 1651), pp. 23 and 27.

destinies they had the privilege to preside. Even when an inconsequential sum was sought to be given for the education of the people, it was subjected to unnecessary legal quibblings and its utilisation was decided on, by and large, extra-educational considerations. Well up to the end of the 19th century, the Government of India fought shy of direct administration of education and insisted upon a policy of gradual withdrawal from education. The university institutions, that were established during this period, were mainly examining bodies, mostly dependent upon examination fees for their maintenance. In the early twentieth century, however, the central and the provincial governments evinced greater interest in the financing of higher education. The transfer of education to popular ministers appointed under the 'Dyarchy' and later on under the Government of India Act, 1935, was expected to improve the financial position of education as well as higher education, but the two economic depressions, which occurred between 1919-24 and 1929-32 forced the provincial governments to economise on educational expenditure. The Second World War (1939-45) added to the financial difficulties of the Government of India and the provincial governments, thus seriously affecting development of education on sound lines.

Notwithstanding the financial and administrative problems facing higher education during the British regime, the period under review witnessed the evolution of some important policies and procedures, which have relevance to the financing of higher education in the present times. The efforts relating to local resource mobilisation by the provincial governments, the evolution of the system of grant-in-aid for educational institutions and the emphasis on the encouragement of private enterprise in higher education are some of the significant features of the history of educational finance, which transcend the limits of time and can still help us in developing policies and procedures of higher educational finance in the present-day India.

NOTES AND REFERENCES

1. A.S. Altekar, *Education in Ancient India* (Varanasi, Anand Kishore, 1965), p. 83.
2. Ved Mitra, *Education in Ancient India*, New Delhi, 1964, p. 48.
3. S.K. Das, *The Educational System of the Ancient Hindus*, Calcutta, 1933, p. 410.
4. Ibid., p. 410.
5. Radha Kumud Mookerji, *Ancient Indian Education*, London, Macmillian, Second Edition, 1951, p. 460.
6. Some of the famous universities during the Buddhist period were the Universities of Nalanda, Valabhai, Vikramsila, Jagaddala, Odantapuri and Mithila.
7. Radha Kumud Mookerji, *Ancient Indian Education*, op. cit., p. 558.
8. Ibid., p. 559.
9. Ibid., p. 560.
10. F.E. Keay, *Indian Education in Ancient and Later Times*, London, Oxford University Press, 1954, p. 117.
11. The general apathy towards educational developments under the Company's Rule in India was described to have been influenced by the British educational tradition of those times. It was argued that if "English could get on without a State organisation, there seemed little reason to introduce one in India and the Company was, at first, a trading rather than a ruling corporation". For this view see, H. Sharp, *Selections from Educational Records*, (*Part I*) (1781-1839), Calcutta, 1920, p. 2-3.
12. In a Despatch of 1659, the Court of Directors had declared their "earnest desire by all possible means to propagate the gospel. Missionaries were allowed to embark on their ships. . ." *Selections*

from Educational Records, op. cit., p. 7. It was only after the Battle of Plassey (1757) on the assumptions of wider powers by the Company that the policy was reversed, and strict "religious neutrality" was declared in regard to educational matters.

13. Warren Hastings, the Governor-General, founded the Calcutta Madrassa with the special object of qualifying "the sons of Mohammadan gentlemen for responsible and lucrative offices in the State, even at that date largely monopolised by the Hindus". (*Source*: *Selections from Educational Records* (Part I) op. cit., p. 7).
14. East India Company Act of 1813—Section 43, Quoted in *Selection from Educational Records*, (Part I) op. cit., p. 22.
15. Macaulay's analysis of the problem and the conclusions arrived at by him merits reproduction. He said: "The question now before us is simply whether, when it is in our power to teach this (English) language, we shall teach languages in which, by universal confession, there are no books in any subject, which deserves to be compared to our own; whether, when we can teach European science, we shall teach systems which, by universal confession, whereas they differ from those of Europe, differ for the worse; and whether when we can patronise sound philosophy and true history, we shall coutenance, at the public expense, medical doctrines, which would disgrace an English farrier—astronomy which would move laughter in girls at an English boarding school—history, abounding with kings thirty feet long and reigns thirty thousand years long and geography made up of seas of treacle and seas of butter" (Macaulay's, *Minutes on Education in India* written in the year 1855, 1836 and 1837 and now first collected from records in the Department of Public Instruction); by H. Woodrow, Calcutta, 1862, p. 138.

    It may be mentioned that H.T. Prinsep in his note dated 15th February, 1835, prepared a point-by-point reply to the assertions made by Macaulay, and described Macaulay's minute as a "partisan paper advocating in a controversial and not very moderate tone, the cause of one section of the Committee" (H. Sharp, *Selections from Educational Records*, op cit., p. 137). Prinsep was, however, over-ruled and rebuked "for having taken upon myself so much", accompanied by the declaration that secretaries are the organs and not advisers of the Government and that their submitting notes was under sufferance and an irregularity" (Ibid., p. 138).
16. Macaulay's, *Minutes on Education in India*, op. cit., pp. 104-116.
17. Ibid., p. 104-116.
18. Lord Bentick's, Resolution of the 17th March, 1835; quoted in H. Sharp, *Selections from Educational Records*, op. cit., p. 130.
19. H. Sharp, *Selection from Educational Report*, Part II, 1840-1859, op. cit., p. 143.
20. J.A. Richey, *Selections from Educational Records*, Part II, 1840-1859; Bureau of Education, India, Calcutta, 1922, p. 1.

21. *Selections from Educational Records*, op. cit., p. 29.
22. Selections from the Records of the Government of India; Home Department, No. IXXVI; A Collection of Despatches from the Home Government on the Subject of Education in India, 1854 to 1868, Calcutta, 1870, p. 1.
23. Ibid., p. 13.
24. Ibid., p. 14.
25. Ibid., p. 15.
26. Ibid., p. 13.
27. The Government of India, vide their Resolution dated October 23, 1884, accepted the policy enunciated by the Commission because of the pecuniary advantages that higher education holds and because of the Government's insistence on the fullest development of a policy of self-help.
28. Report of the Indian Education Commission appointed by the Resolution of the Government of India, Calcutta, 1883, p. 305.
29. Ibid., p. 308.
30. *Indian Education Commission*, op. cit., pp. 433-39.
31. *Progress of Education in India*, 1897-98—1901-02, Vol. I, Calcutta, 1904, p. 4.
32. Eric Ashby, (in association with Mary Anderson), *Universities: British, Indian, African—A Study in the Ecology of Higher Education*, London, Weidenfield and Nicolson, p. 73.
33. *Lord Curzon in India—1898-1905*, London, Macmillan and Co. Ltd.; 1906, Part II, p. 33-34.
34. Report of the Indian Universities Commission, Simla, 1902, p. 17.
35. Indian Educational Policy—being a Resolution issued by the Governor-General in Council on the 11th March, 1904, Calcutta, 1904, p. 13-14.
36. Ibid., p. 14.
37. Quoted in the Indian Educational Policy, 1913; being a Resolution issued by the Governor-General in Council on the 21st February, 1913, Calcutta, 1913, p. 1.
38. Ibid., p. 20-21.
39. H.W. Orange, *Progress of Education in India, 1902-1907*, Fifth Quinquennial Review, Vol. I, Calcutta, 1909, p. 30.
40. Government of India, Department of Education, Indian Education in 1913-14, Calcutta, India, 1915, p. 11.
41. Calcutta University Commission, Vol. V (Part II) Calcutta, India, 1919, p. 240.
42. R. Little Hailes, *Progress of Education in India, 1922-27*, Ninth Quinquennial Review, Vol. I: Calcutta, 1929, p. 2.
43. Interim Report of the Indian Statutory Commission; (Review of the Growth of Education in British India by the Auxiliary Committee appointed by the Commission), September, 1929, (Printed in India, London), p. 276.

44. John Sargent, *Progress of Education in India, 1932-37*, Eleventh Quinquennial Review, Vol. I, Simla, 1940, p. 1.
45. Interim Report of the Indian Statutory Commission, op. cit., p. 278-79.
46. John Sargent, Post-War Educational Development in India, Report by the Central Advisory Board of Education, Bureau of Education, India, New Delhi, 1944, p. 97.
47. Ibid., p. 33.
48. Ibid., p. 34.
49. J.A. Richey, *Progress of Education in India, 1917-22*, Eighth Quinquennial Review, Vol. I, Calcutta, 1923, p. 2.
50. Ibid., p. 30.

3

STATE GRANTS
General Conditions

WE HAVE already referred to the heterogeneity of the system of higher education under which institutions with vast financial and material resources co-exist with institutions eking out a miserable existence. To the latter category belong the affiliated colleges which, notwithstanding the fact that they account for about 83 per cent of student enrolment, appear to be nobody's concern. These colleges have mushroomed, in spite of the regulatory measures adopted by some state governments and the universities, giving rise to the "general feeling in India that the situation in higher education is unsatisfactory and even alarming in some ways; that the average standards have been falling and that the rapid expansion has resulted in lowering quality. . .".[1]

In this chapter, we shall examine the general conditions laid down by the state governments, federal agencies and the universities to regulate the growth of these institutions as also to provide financial sustenance for their maintenance and development.

STATE GOVERNMENTS AND UNIVERSITIES

A majority of state governments have laid down elaborate rules governing the setting up of managing bodies, creation of reserve fund, qualifications of teachers, enrolment, tuition fees as also whether or not the teachers should take part in politics. Quite a few states have, however, left the question open, leaving the decision to the state bureaucracy. All the universities have prescribed conditions of affiliation of collegiate institutions, which mainly relate to academic matters. There are also some regulations about the physical infra-structure as a condition precedent for academic affiliation by the universities.

The private bodies have, however, shown extraordinary resilience in that in spite of a myriad of conditions from so many agencies, the pace of institutional proliferation has been going on unabated. It is another matter that almost half of these institutions are 'non-viable', having little potentiality for academic growth, according to the norms set out by the U.G.C.

The general conditions of grants to private colleges will be examined in the following order:

(i) A descriptive analysis of the important conditions laid down by the different state governments and the universities; and

(ii) a critical examination of these conditions keeping in view the observations made by the collegiate institutions and universities, who were requested to give their reactions to specific conditions as also to make suggestions for improving the system.

A descriptive analysis

The conditions for grant-in-aid laid down by the state governments and the universities could be broadly grouped under the following categories:

(a) Administrative;
(b) Financial; and
(c) Academic.

A discussion of the important conditions follows.

Administrative

Institutional proliferation

To regulate unplanned proliferation of collegiate institutions, particularly of humanities and social sciences, a few state governments have framed rules governing the opening of colleges. For example, the Tamil Nadu Government has forbidden the establishment of any private college without the permission of the competent authority.[2] This stipulation does not apply to minority colleges. In Haryana, the opening of the colleges is subject to the issue of a no-objection certificate from the state government. The Government of Madhya Pradesh does not sanction any grant to an institution, if it is found to be unnecessary or unsuited to the requirements of the locality.[3] The Government of Gujarat has set up a Board, which decides whether a new college should or should not be located at a given place.[4] Quite a number of states, however, consider it prudent to adopt a policy of benign neutrality and allow the private bodies to have a free play of their acquisitive instincts.

Managing/governing body

Almost all the states, which grant assistance for the collegiate institutions, insist that the colleges should be under regularly constituted managements, which should be registered bodies. It has been further laid down that the state assistance would be admissible only to an institution, which is affiliated to a statutory university. Nine States, Haryana, Jammu and Kashmir, Karnataka, Madhya Pradesh, Punjab, Rajasthan, Orissa, Tamil Nadu and West Bengal insist upon the secular character of the institution. A perusal of the university Acts reveals that almost all the universities insist upon regularly constituted managing bodies for the colleges.

Participation in political activities

The Governments of Andhra Pradesh, Assam, Jammu and Kashmir, Karnataka, Kerala, Madhya Pradesh and West Bengal have debarred the teachers/students from participating in political agitations. The Government of Andhra Pradesh insists that a member of the aid-receiving colleges shall not stand as a candidate or interfere with or use his influence in any way or do anything in aid or in obstruction of any candidate in any election to a legislature or a local authority whether in India or elsewhere; nor shall he take part or subscribe in aid of any electioneering party organisation. The

Government of Jammu and Kashmir forbids the institutions to indulge in any 'unhealthy' activities of a political nature. The Governments of Kerala, Tamil Nadu, Karnataka and Madhya Pradesh refuse financial assistance, if the manager of any private institution or any teacher employed by him takes part in a political agitation directed against the authority of the government or inculcates opinions tending to excite feelings of disloyalty or disaffection among the students. The Government of Karnataka has debarred its employees from engaging themselves in any demonstration prejudicial to the soverignty and integrity of India, the security of the State, decency or morality, and so on. They will also not associate themselves with any political party or organisation or take part in any political movement. They are also debarred from contesting elections to the state legislature, local authority or Parliament. Similar restrictions have been placed on the managements who are disallowed to take part in any political agitation directed against the authority of the state government or foster opinion tending to excite feeling of disloyalty or disaffection among the students.

Religious neutrality

By and large, the state grant-in-aid rules are based on religious neutrality. Jammu and Kashmir State has laid down that religious instruction shall be voluntary. The Government of Madhya Pradesh disallows any grant to denominational or sectarian institutions. The Governments of Orissa, Tamil Nadu and West Bengal have also framed rules to discourage sectarian propaganda in educational institutions. The Governments of Kerala and Tamil Nadu refuse grant-in-aid, if the institution directly or indirectly encourages propaganda to bring into ridicule or contempt the beliefs and practices of any religion. The Punjab Government disallows any grant to institutions which foster communal activities.

Discipline

The Governments of Punjab, Rajasthan and West Bengal insist upon discipline among students as a pre-condition for state grants. The Governments of Haryana and Punjab insist upon the good character of its teachers. The Government of Assam forbids its teachers to accept any office not connected with college work without the prior approval of the Government.

Reservation for weaker sections

The Kerala and Madhya Pradesh Governments refuse grant, if the institutions do not reserve seats for Scheduled Castes/ Scheduled Tribes in colleges.

Financial

Probationary period

In a number of states, the collegiate institutions have to pass through a *probationary* period, which may extend to 9 years! During this period, the institutions are qenerally not eligible for any state assistance.

Definition of 'approved' expenditure

The assistance from the state governments is available generally on the basis of the 'deficit' expenditure, which in state terminology means 'approved' income minus 'approved' expenditure. Almost all the states have specified what constitutes the 'approved' income and expenditure. A perusal of the items constituting 'approved' expenditure, however, reveals substantial variations among the various states. In some states even such items as water and electricity charges, telephone bills, annual repairs of buildings, playgrounds and so on are excluded from the definition of approved expenditure.

Reserve fund

In Jammu and Kashmir State, the institutions seeking government assistance are required to create a reserve fund, which should not be less than their normal expenditure for six months The Government of Orissa insists that the college should have a fixed deposit of Rs. 2 lakhs for arts or commerce courses and Rs. 2.50 lakhs for science courses. The amount has to be pledged to the university. Quite a few other states have also stipulated conditions for the creation of a reserve fund. The stipulation is, however, somewhat vague. For example, the government of Tripura has laid down that the college should have "adequate income from endowment and other sources." The extent of adequacy has, however, not been defined.

Out of the 50 universities, whose Acts were examined, 42 universities have laid down conditions about the adequacy of the financial resources with the institutions seeking affiliation to the universities. The stipulation has, however, been imprecisely worded: 23 universities have laid down that the financial resources of the college seeking affiliation should be such as to ensure its continued and efficient working. A few other universities insist upon 'adequate' financial resources. Only three universities, Jiwaji (Gwalior), Bihar (Patna) and Punjab (Chandigarh) have specified the quantum of amount to be provided as reserve fund.

Fees

The grant-in-aid rules generally provide that the rates of fees and other levies should be approved by the state government. Some state governments, however, allow the colleges to levy higher fees with the permission of the government. The Government of Gujarat, while laying down uniform tuition fees for colleges of general education, has stipulated that in case a college levies higher fees, the extra amount should be utilised for developmental purposes. In the case of technical education, the Government of Gujarat allows the institutions to charge higher rates of fees to the extent of 50 per cent with the approval of the director of technical education and still higher rates with the approval of the government. The Government of Karnataka permits the managements to collect tuition fees and laboratory fees at rates not exceeding twice the standard rates prescribed by the Government. The Tamil Nadu Government disallows the levying of fees other than those prescribed by the competent authority. The colleges charging different fees from those prescribed by the competent authority are required to obtain the prior approval of the authority before introducing tuition fees at enhanced rates. The Government of Kerala allows the management to collect special fees, besides tuition fees at rates prescribed by the university. This is to be remitted in the separate account to be utilised only for the purpose for which they have been collected. The Government of Punjab does not allow any deviation from the government rules prescribing fees and concessions. The Government of Rajasthan allows charging of fees at higher rates than those in government institutions but excludes the excess income from the income of the institution.

Most of the university acts have laid down conditions about charging of fees. The important stipulations are that the fixing of fees should not involve any competition with any existing institution in the neighbourhood and that it should not be injurious to the cause of education. The Kerala, Ranchi and Karnataka universities acts stipulate that the fees should be in accordance with the amounts specified in the act/ordinance or approved by the syndicate. The Punjab University Act has warned the colleges against adopting commercial practices. Sri Venkateswara University has disallowed any levy on the teaching staff for instituting scholarships or meeting its general and special needs.

Limits on surplus funds

Some state governments, like Maharashtra, Gujarat and Karnataka, have laid down that no grant-in-aid will be allowed if the management has a surplus of Rs. 1 lakh or more in hand.

Academic

Staff

tates like Andhra Pradesh, Assam, Kerala, Karnataka and 'amil Nadu have laid down maximum age limit for teachers 'hich, except in Tamil Nadu, is 60 years. Most of the state overnments have inserted rules about the salary scales of :achers. The general stipulation is that the payment of grants 'ill be subject to the provision of salary scales and dearness lowance as prescribed by the government. A number of ates: Andhra Pradesh, Gujarat, Karnataka, Kerala, Iaharashtra, Orissa and U.P. have introduced a system of rect payment of salaries to the teachers.

The Tamil Nadu Government has stipulated that no teacher nployed in any private college shall be dismissed, removed reduced in rank nor shall his appointment be otherwise terminated except with the prior approval of the competent authority. Madhya Pradesh also forbids the college managements to terminate the services of the teachers without holding full inquiry into the charges against him and giving him full opportunity to defend himself according to the principle of natural justice

In almost all university acts, it has been laid down that the strength, qualifications and conditions of service of the teaching and non-teaching staff should be such as to make due provisions for courses of instruction undertaken by the college.

Enrolment

Some of the State Governments have laid down conditions of enrolment in order to make the colleges eligible for grant-in-aid. For example, Assam insists upon 300 students in degree colleges for arts and 120 for science courses. Gujarat, on the basis of the recommendations of the Committee on College Finances appointed by the State Government, has stipulated that the maximum enrolment should be 1,650 which may be raised to 2,000 in a three-faculty college with the approval of the university. In the case of colleges located in cities with a population of one lakh and above, the minimum enrolment should be 300, 500 and 700 in single, double and triple-faculty colleges respectively. The corresponding figures for colleges in cities with a population of less than one lakh or in rural areas should be 200, 350 and 500 respectively.[5] The Government of Maharashtra has also laid down varying enrolments for different regions depending upon the population of the respective areas.

Assam and Jammu and Kashmir insist upon good results in university examinations.

FEDERAL AGENCIES

The most important federal agency for the affiliated colleges is the University Grants Commission. The Commission's assistance is primarily for the development of the institution rather than its maintenance. The Commission has, therefore, laid down criteria for determining the viability of a college

With this end in view, the Commission gives due consideration to the following aspects:

(a) Social and educational needs of the community in which the college is located;
(b) the capacity of the institution to maintain standards and to provide instructional facilities; and
(c) academic viability rather than financial, managerial or other considerations.

The commission has, accordingly, adopted the following criteria for determining viability in respect of arts, science and multi-faculty colleges:

(i) There should be at least four departments in the college, with at least two teachers in each department;
(ii) there should be at least ten permanent teachers excluding the principal and the physical education teacher;
(iii) the overall student teacher ratio in the college should not exceed 20 : 1; and
(iv) the college should have at least 300 students in degree classes and above (beyond plus two stage); this is relaxable to 200 in the case of women's colleges and colleges in backward/rural areas.

A critical examination

It would be observed that the main thrust of the conditions imposed by the state governments is on administrative and financial aspects rather than on academic improvement of the institutions. In the absence of any empirical evidence, it is difficult to vouchsafe the effectiveness or otherwise of the conditions in ensuring a harmonious growth of institutions of higher education. The unrestricted mushrooming of collegiate institutions, however, testifies to the lack of seriousness on the part of the universities and the state governments to enforce these regulations. The general practice seems to be for the enterprising private bodies to initiate action about the setting up of collegiate institutions, admit students and then to present the state governments and the universities with a *fait accompli.* As a consequence, "many colleges spring up because of non-academic considerations like political pressures and parochial rivalries and without adequate previous preparation and with little financial support. . . ".[7]

Institutional reactions

The university institutions were requested to give their views about some of the important conditions of state grants. They were also requested to indicate the manner in which these rules needed modification. The responses of these institutions are summarised below.

Need for modification

To a general question whether there was need for modifying the conditions of grants, 63 per cent of the collegiate institutions, who were approached, responded in the affirmative. The universities were, however, less enthusiastic; only 40 per cent pleaded for modification. This is, however, understandable because the universities are governed by more liberal conditions of grants and hence their reaction is not as pointed as that of the colleges.

Specific responses

In view of the varying character of the conditions of grants, the responses of the institutions in different states are quite often at variance with one another. A perusal of the institutional responses shows that, except in the case of Bihar, Punjab, Tamil Nadu and U.P., the institutions in other states have made detailed suggestions about modifying the conditions of grants. Quite a few responses are non-quantifiable because of their being at variance with one another. The following may be said by way of institutional responses to certain specific conditions:

Salary scales of teachers

A large majority of the institutions (about 80%) have suggested that the salary scales of teachers should accord with those of their counterparts in government institutions. Almost all engineering and technical institutions have also insisted on this stipulation. Sixty per cent of the university institutions have endorsed this suggestion.

Should the institutions be allowed to fix their own scales of pay? To this, the response of the majority of institutions was in the negative. Only about 17 per cent of the responding institutions agreed to this suggestion. As for the institutions of technical education, a little more than half agreed to this suggestion. By far the largest majority of the university institutions (84%) disagreed with this suggestion.

While it would be agreed that the salary scales of teachers in government and private institutions should be similar, there appears to be no harm in allowing these institutions to raise the salary scales of teachers in case they can provide the additional funds required for this purpose out of their own resources. This will enable them to attract better qualified teachers to their institutions. Care should, however, be taken that better remuneration for teachers is not at the cost of other infrastructural facilities.

Participation of students/teachers in politics

The percentage of university institutions favouring the participation of students/teachers in politics is indicated below:

Type of the institution	*Percentage favouring*
Colleges of general education	7.9
Colleges of technical education	11.1
All colleges	8.3
Universities	0.0
All institutions	7.1

It may be concluded that an overwhelming majority of the responding institutions do not support the participation of students/teachers in politics.

While there is no dispute about banning teachers' participation in active politics, the extension of this embargo even to a theoretical discussion of politics is likely to be abused by the government. It will also lead to a stifling of the intellect of the teachers and students. The policy should be that the teachers should actively involve themselves in theoretical discussion of the political events and their impact on the socio-economic system. They should, however, not fritter away their energies in associating themselves actively with the political parties. The real trouble starts when the students and teachers divide themselves on the basis of the main political parties in the country and allow themselves to be led by the politicians, who use them for their petty political ends.

Quantum of reserve fund

The institutions have made suggestions about the need for having a reserve fund of varying dimensions. The quantum varies from Rs. 15,000 suggested by one institution in Punjab to Rs. 5 lakhs suggested by an institution in Maharashtra. The institutions in Orissa have suggested different quantum of reserve fund for science and arts colleges. The only institution that responded to this question in Tamil Nadu suggested that the quantum of reserve fund should be 15 times the net deficit of an institution. One institution in West Bengal suggested reserve fund equal to six months' salary.

Libraries and laboratories

Under this head also, some vague suggestions have been made about the need to have 'well-equipped' libraries and laboratories. Only some institutions in Madhya Pradesh suggested purchase of books worth Rs. 5,000 to Rs. 50,000. The other suggestions are: "adequate" and "spacious" laboratories, "extensive" playgrounds and so on. These suggestions are, obviously, too ambiguous to be of much help.

Other conditions

A recurrent theme has been that the period of 'probation', that is, the period during which the institutions have to wait to receive state assistance, should be reduced, if not eliminated altogether. An institution in Andhra Pradesh has suggested reduction of this period from five to two years. The regular payment of salary to the staff and adequate representation of the staff on the managing body has also been stressed. The need for providing medical and other benefits like pensions and so on as available to the government servants has been underlined. The institutions in Kerala have suggested that staff selection committees should include representatives of the universities and the state government. Some institutions have suggested that the financial viability of the institutions should be ensured. It has been further suggested that no capitation fees should be charged and that no donation should be expected of the staff.

Definition of 'approved' expenditure

As stated earlier, the list of items included in the 'approved' expenditure varies substantially from state to state. The institutions were, therefore, requested to indicate:

(a) Whether the list of approved expenditure pertaining to their state was comprehensive enough to include all the essential items; and

(b) if it did not include all the essential items, the institutions might indicate the items that needed to be added to the list.

The analysis of responses from the institutions reveals that, by and large, the institutions are not satisfied with the list of items of approved expenditure prescribed by the state governments. Considered on an all-India basis, hardly one out of four collegiate institutions (27.8%) and slightly less proportion of universities (24%) expressed their satisfaction with the lists prescribed by the states.

The institutions have suggested a variety of items of approved expenditure for inclusion in the list in different states. Some of them are: compound wall, buildings, playgrounds, furniture, water supply, electricity, telephone charges, annual repairs of buildings, research, experimentation publications, medical aid to members of the families of staff, college campus maintenance, libraries, student trips, laboratories, printing and sationery, and so on.

As a general conclusion, it may be stated that quite a number of essential items, which have a bearing on the standards of educational facilities provided by the institutions, do not find a place in the list of approved items of expenditure and are hence ineligible for state assistance. If, in the process, the institutions are unable to provide these essential facilities adequately, the reasons would not be far to seek.

NOTES AND RFFERENCES

1. Education Commission (1964-66), Government of India, p. 503.
2. Tamil Nadu Private Colleges (Regulation) Ordinance, 1976, p.57.
3. Grant-in-aid Rules for Non-government Institutions of Higher Education (Technical) in Madhya Pradesh, Mimeo. p. 2.
4. This has been done in pursuance of the recommendations of the Committee on College Finances, 1977. Ahmedabad. (See p. 7 of the Report).
5. Ibid, p. 49.
6. See U.G.C. Annual Reports for 1979-80, 1980-81 and 1981-82, p. 14.
7. Report of the Committee on Colleges; UGC, New Delhi, 1967. p. 14.

4

STATE GRANTS
Patterns and Procedures

THE STATE government grants to universities and colleges could be broadly grouped under three categories:

(i) Maintenance grants, which are basically for the day-to-day functioning of the institutions;
(ii) development grants, which are given mainly on a matching basis to enable the institutions to lift the assistance given by the federal agencies like the U.G.C., I.C.A.R., etc.; and
(iii) non-recurring grants for buildings, equipments, etc.

COLLEGES OF GENERAL EDUCATION

A summary of the different types of grants admissible to colleges of general education and technical education is given in the annexure. A summary statement is given at the end of this Chapter. The following broad features may be specially mentioned in respect of colleges of general education:

Maintenance grants
The maintenance grants vary from less than 50 per cent of the net deficit in West Bengal to 100 per cent of the net deficit in Andhra Pradesh, Assam, Jammu and Kashmir, Madhya Pradesh and West Bengal (for government sponsored colleges only). Four States—Tamil Nadu, Tripura, Punjab and Rajasthan give grants between 70 and 95 per cent of the

approved expenditure. The Orissa Government's grants escalate from 33 per cent after 5 years to 100 per cent after 9 years of the colleges being brought on the list of government assisted institutions. West Bengal gives assistance to the extent of 50 per cent of the net deficit or Rs. 30,000 whichever is less. Seven States—Andhra Pradesh, Gujarat, Karnataka, Kerala, Maharashtra, Orissa and Uttar Pradesh have introduced the system of paying salaries directly to the teachers. The practices, however, very substantially from state to state. In the case of Andhra Pradesh, for example, all the colleges having 80 per cent aided posts have been brought under the salary payment scheme through the banks. In Kerala, a system of direct payment of salaries has been introduced. Four States—Bihar, Himachal Pradesh, Nagaland and Punjab—have framed no rules about giving maintenance grants.

The system introduced by Rajasthan and Gujarat deserve a special mention. In Rajasthan, the private colleges have been classified into four categories: A, B, C and D, which are given grants-in-aid of 80, 70, 60 and 50 per cent, respectively, of the expenditure of the previous year plus likely annual increments to staff. Besides these four categories, there is a special category of colleges eligible for assistance to the extent of 90 per cent of the net deficit. It has, however, been laid down that the total recurring grants shall not exceed the difference between the total approved expenditure and income from fees and other sources during the same year excluding grants from state and central governments, sabhas, societies and local bodies.

Gujarat State has introduced the system of pay packet grant besides the developmental grants for the schemes sponsored by the U.G.C. The state government has also introduced 'performance grant' under which every college is expected to introduce a system of institutional planning on the basis of over-all comprehensive assessment of their progress in academic and extra-curricular activities. Judged on this basis, the first three colleges are eligible for performance awards of Rs. 1,00,000, Rs. 75,000 and Rs. 50,000, respectively. The performance has to be evaluated by the Gujarat Affiliated Colleges Board. Besides, special grants for providing special tuition and guidance to scheduled castes and scheduled tribes are also available. All these grants are subject to colleges having enrolments of varying dimensions specified by the government.

Building grants

The general pattern is 50 per cent of the expenditure. Some states have, however, no system of grants for buildings and equipments. These are Assam, Bihar, Haryana, Himachal Pradesh, Kerala, Karnataka, Nagaland and Uttar Pradesh. Invariably, the state governments have laid down financial limits for building grants. For example, both Andhra Pradesh and Tamil Nadu have laid down a limit of Rs. 75,000 for first grade colleges and Rs. 50,000 for second grade colleges. Tripura has fixed a limit of Rs. 2 lakhs.

Equipment and other grants

Here also the general trend is to meet 50 per cent of the cost. Some states, however, have introduced rules of assistance, which indicate a policy of selective discrimination. For example, Madhya Pradesh gives 75 per cent assistance for science laboratories; Maharashtra gives monetary assistance to the tune of Rs. 30 per science student; Tamil Nadu's assistance is limited to the maximum of Rs. 10,000; Punjab gives a special grant of Rs. 3,000 each for colleges for women and in rural areas.

COLLEGES OF TECHNICAL EDUCATION

Maintenance grants

Except for Andhra Pradesh, which gives grant of 65 per cent of the approved expenditure for boys' polytechnics, the assistance provided by other states varies between 75 and 100 per cent of the approved expenditure. Kerala and U.P. have introduced the system of direct payment to teachers. Assam, Bihar, Himachal Pradesh, Nagaland, Orissa, Rajasthan and Madhya Pradesh have not specified the pattern of assistance.

Building and equipment grants

Andhra Pradesh, Haryana, Kerala and Madhya Pradesh provide assistance which is less than 50 per cent of the cost of the building. Karnataka and Tamil Nadu's assistance is more than 50 per cent. In the case of the remaining states, no specific regulations have been made. The general pattern of equipment grants is to lay down monetary limits. For example, Karnataka gives 50 per cent assistance subject to a maximum limit of Rs. 50,000 for engineering colleges and Rs. 20,000 for polytechnics. Kerala provides assistance at the rate of Rs. 3,000 and Rs, 1,000 respectively to colleges and polytechnics. Grants are also available for libraries and laboratories. U.P. gives assistance for contingent expenditure at the rate of Rs. 165 per student.

STATE GRANTS TO UNIVERSITIES

The state government grants to state universities may be broadly classified into the following categories:

(a) Statutory grants like the foundation fund/endowment fund etc.
(b) maintenance grants/block grants, which are determined for a specified period ranging from 3 to 5 years and released on an annual basis.
(c) development grants which include provision of matching contribution in respect of U.G.C. schemes.

Statutory grants

Out of 53 universities, which supplied information, 23 universities were in receipt of statutory/foundation grants. These grants ranged between as low as Rs. 2 lakhs each in the cases of Berhampur and Sambalpur Universities in Orissa to about Rs. 226 lakhs in the case of Pant Agricultural University in Uttar Pradesh. Only in the case of 3 other universities (Meerut Punjab and Kerala Agricultural) the amount of foundation/statutory grant exceeded Rs. 50 lakhs. In one case (Saurashtra University) the state government had contented itself by giving a piece of land for the university campus.

Maintenance grants

These grants are determined by the state governments for a specified period ranging from 3 to 5 years. These grants are subject to an increase on account of enhancement in salaries of staff and other escalations in costs. The grants are determined on the basis of the following criteria:

(i) The net deficit of the university on approved items for the previous year plus some increase on account of the rise in costs; and
(ii) the budgetary constraints of the state government.

Development grants
Development grants are given by the state governments in order to enable the universities to lift the U.G.C.'s assistance or assistance from the Ministry of Health/Indian Council of Agricultural Research, in respect of departments of medicine and agriculture respectively. The states also give development grants for schemes sponsored by them.

A CRITICAL EXAMINATION OF THE SYSTEM

The professed objective of government grants is to help the university institutions achieve their optimum development. It is difficult to realise these aims unless the grant-in-aid system satisfies the criteria of equity and efficiency and so on. More precisely, the system of state grants, in order to be an effective instrument of integrated development of university institutions, should be in consonance with the following basic principles:

Equity
The system should not be discriminatory in that it should not give preferential treatment to one set of institutions against the others unless it is warranted by special circumstances and needs of the institution.

Specificity
The system should be specific in the sense that it should allocate specific responsibilities to the different agencies that finance higher education. Further, it should not be vague and imprecise in interpretation.

Adequacy
The system should ensure adequate assistance for the maintenance and development of university institutions.

Elasticity
A good system of grant-in-aid should be elastic to stand the stresses and strains that arise over a period of time.

Promotional
It should encourage the institutions to: (i) improve their academic standard by faculty improvement programmes, (ii) developing physical infrastructure and (iii) mobilising financial resources for the development of the institutions.

Efficiency
It should be efficient in administration.

Academic freedom
It should respect the academic freedom of the institution.

The grant-in-aid system, as operating at present for the universities and colleges, is examined below in terms of the above-mentioned parameters:

Equity
The principle of equity implies that the system of grant-in-aid should be applicable uniformly to all types of institutions. The underlying idea is that once the need for a collegiate institution has been recognised, the state should help it to grow to its optimum capacity. At that stage, consideration of the type and location of institutions, the courses of study offered, and so on should not be relevant factors for providing financial assistance.

A perusal of grant-in-aid rules in different states reveals that the system is somewhat inequitable in that certain types of institutions are given grants on a more liberal scale than others. For example, the universities and professional colleges are, by and large, among the most favoured institutions as against the colleges of general education, which do not seem to be of much concern to the central or state governments. In some states, distinction is made between arts and science colleges.

The wide variations in the patterns of grants introduced by different states bring out the inter-state discrimination perpetrated on collegiate institutions. For example, in same states, the colleges of general education have to be content with the state meeting one-third of their approved expenditure. In some others, they are favoured with grants equivalent to as much as 100 per cent of the deficit expenditure. In still some other states, the system of salary grants has been introduced.

There are wide variations in the interpretation of 'approved' expenditure by different state governments. As would be explained in a subsequent paragraph, some states do not include certain essential items such as telephone charges, repairs to buildings and so on among the 'approved' items of expenditure and hence they are ineligible for state assistance.

Specificity

The system of grant-in-aid introduced by the state governments lacks specificity on account of the following factors:

(a) A number of state governments like, Bihar, Haryana, Himachal Pradesh, Nagaland and Punjab have not laid down any specific proportion of expenditure to be paid as state grants. The grant-in-aid is, therefore, determined by the state bureaucracy, which may not be able to appreciate adequately the financial requirements of the colleges.

(b) as already stated, in a number of states, the terms 'approved' income and expenditure have not been clearly defined with the result that the state governments decide the quantum of assistance on the basis of the ad-hoc norms laid down for the purpose from time to time.

(c) even when the percentage of expenditure admissible for grant-in-aid from the state governments has been laid down, the actual quantum of assistance to be made available to the institutions may be at variance with these norms. An important causative factor in this is the stipulation by most of the state governments that state grants shall not be claimed as a matter of right and that the actual availabilty of grants for institutions of higher education would be subject to the availability of funds. This means that the institutions have to be given assistance subject to the exigencies of the financial situation operating at the given point of time.

(d) The prescribed pattern of grants may prove to be illusory in some states because of the arbitrary financial ceilings imposed on certain schemes of assistance. For example, in a number of states, the assistance for buildings and equipments is prescribed as 50 per cent of the expenditure. The actual assistance cannot, however, exceed a fixed financial limit. For instance, in Andhra Pradesh, the first grade colleges are eligible for 50 per cent assistance for buildings, subject to a maximum of Rs. 75,000. The financial ceiling for second grade colleges is Rs. 50,000. In Karnataka, the engineering institutions are eligible for 50 per cent state assistance subject to a maximnm limit of Rs. 50,000 for engineering colleges and Rs. 20,000 for polytechnics.

(e) It has also been observed that the different grant-giving bodies have tended to work in isolation, without consulting one another to evolve the best manner in which the much-needed finances could be provided to university institutions. The main grant-giving body at the central level like the U.G.C., at least in the initial stages, did not consider it necessary to consult the state governments about the financial implications of the schemes floated by the former and the part that the states have to play in making these programmes a success. Very often, the U.G.C. announced schemes of financial assistance to the universities and colleges, which were more in the nature of 'take it' or 'leave it'. Sometimes, the schemes were announced in the mid year, when the state budgets had been passed and there was hardly any scope for adjustments to accommodate the new schemes.

The lack of specificity is also discernible from the absence of any clear demarcation of financial responsibility between the central and the state governments. Both the governments are financing almost similar schemes of university and college development. This is notwithstanding the fact that the Constitution has laid down specific responsibilities for the central and the state governments. In order to avoid overlapping and eliminate infructuous expenditure, it is imperative that specific responsibilities of the central and the state governments may be agreed upon by mutual consultation. The programmes that are of a local character should be financed by the state governments and the schemes which are important from the point of view of improvement of standards of higher education and which have inter-university and inter-state implications should fall within the purview of the central government acting through the specialised organisations like the UGC, ICAR and so on. In the first category will fall programmes like improvement of salaries of teachers, setting up and maintenance of physical facilities etc. In the latter category will fall schemes like post-graduate education and research provision of costly and sophisticated equipment like computers and scientific appliances and so on.

Adequacy

That the financial provision available with the universities and particularly collegiate institutions of non-professional type is inadequate does not need very complicated statistical analysis. The general lack of educational facilities available with the colleges and universities is an eloquent testimony to the inadequacy of finances with these institutions. The Review Committee of the UGC, which recently examined this question in terms of the grants being made available to the universities by the UGC, came to the conclusion that in a number of cases, the grants by state governments to universities have not been adequate. A number of other committees have also come to the same conclusion.

In order to assess the financial position of the universities from the point of its adequacy, data in respect of 29 universities for 9 years between 1966-67 to 1974-75 was analysed. Cumulative frequencies were worked out in respect of those universities having surplus, deficit or balanced budgets over the years under study. The position has been summarised in Table 4.1 below:

TABLE 4.1 : **Budgetary position of universities**

Universities having	1966-67 to 1974-75 Cumulative frequency	Percentage to total
Balanced budgets	49	18.7
Surplus budgets	88	33.7
Deficit budgets	99	38.0
No information	25	9 6
Total	261	100.0

Source : Data has been taken from the Report of the Review Committee on the UGC, 1977, pp. 148-153.

It would appear that only a little more than half of the universities reported having balanced or surplus budgets. Almost two out of every five universities were having deficit budgets, that is, their expenditure exceeded their income.

It may be mentioned that in the study undertaken by us, the institutions were requested to indicate whether the types and quantum of state grants under various heads were adequate for their maintenance and development. The responses of the collegiate institutions show dissatisfaction with the type and quantum of grants. Fiftyseven per cent of the institutions testified to the inadequacy of maintenance grants.

A similar question was put to the universities also. Only 16 per cent of the universities reported about adequacy of the state grants for their maintenance. The universities were also requested to indicate the steps taken by them to meet the budgetary deficits, in the event of the state grants being inadequate. The typical responses of the universities are summarised below:

(i) Keeping posts vacant;
(ii) not taking up development plans;
(iii) generally restricting expenditure on buildings and equipment; and
(iv) reducing expenditure on games and sports.

The universities were also requested to comment on the adequacy or otherwise of the development grants given by the central and the state governments. Only 16 per cent of the universities expressed their satisfaction with the adequacy of the quantum of development grants from the central government. So far as the development grants from the state governments are concerned, only 12 per cent of the universities and 18 per cent of the colleges testified to their adequacy.

Elasticity

The system of state grants lacks elasticity in that it has been unable to withstand the stresses and strains that arise over a period of time. The system has been under strain because of the rising costs of educational apparatus and the increasing expectations of teachers. The inability of the private organisations to provide the much needed financial support as a matching contribution has also vitiated the system of grant-in-aid. The case in point is the introduction of successive revisions of salary scales of college and university teachers on the recommendations of the UGC or as a result of the pressures exerted by teachers' organisations. This enhanced the financial liability of the private institutions without corresponding increase in government subventions as also private contributions to meet these liabilities. In some cases, the teachers had to agitate over a considerably long period to make the state governments agree to the increase in the salary scales on the recommendations of the UGC. The elasticity of the system of state grants was put to a severe test because of some of the undesirable practices indulged in by some of the management of private colleges. The result was that quite a few states like Gujarat, Karnataka, Kerala and U.P. had to introduce the system of direct payment to teachers. This shows that the system of state grants was not elastic enough to absorb the strains imposed by changing circumstances.

Promotional

As already stated, the promotional role of the system of grants-in-aid can be measured in relation to the following parameters:

(a) its capacity to encourage the institutions to show better results through faculty improvement programmes, building up physical infrastructure; and

(b) providing an inbuilt mechanism to mobilise financial resources.

Considered from these points of view, the procedures of grant-in-aid leave much to be desired. This is borne out by the responses to our questionnaire given by the principals of colleges of the states of Andhra Pradesh, Haryana and Gujarat. The reactions of the principals to various questions about the promotional role of the state grants-in-aid are summarised in Table 4.2 below:

TABLE 4.2 : **Responses of principals of colleges in relation to the promotional role of state government grant-in-aid**

	Percentage responding		Total
	In favour	Against	
Faculty improvement	40	60	100
Restructuring of courses of studies	29	71	100
Developing physical infrastructure	25	75	100
Promoting research	24	76	100
Mobilising financial resources	21	79	100

It would appear that an overwhelming majority of principals of the colleges located in the states mentioned above have testified against the potentiality of the grant-in-aid rules in these states to play a promotional role in the type of academic and extra-academic activities listed above. Some principals have gone to the extent of saying that the state grants are just enough to "run the show" and provide little incentives for the activities mentioned above.

As already mentioned, some states are awakening to the need of giving some incentives for better performance. Notable among them are Rajasthan and Gujarat. Rajasthan has framed rules of giving higher grants to institutions, which have been classified as better institutions. The Government of Gujarat has also introduced a system of performance grants, under which it is expected that every college would introduce a system of institutional planning on the basis of overall comprehensive assessment of their progress in academic and extra-curricular activities.

So far as mobilisation of community resources by the institutions of higher education is concerned, the position is far from satisfactory. Not only that the state grant-in-aid rules do not provide much incentives to the colleges for mobilising financial resources, in some states the grant-in-aid rules, in effect, mititate against the mobilisation of resources. For example, in the case of Maharashtra, no grant is paid to a college with a surplus or balance in hand including that of the previous years of Rs. 1 lakh and over. Further, most of the states have laid down that the institutions cannot raise tuition fees. Only in a few states, the state governments permit the collegiate institutions to charge higher fees. The fees are an important source of university finances and a moratorium on them would be detrimental to the mobilisation of financial resources.

Efficiency

The extent of efficiency in the administration of the system of grant-in-aid has a direct bearing on the effectiveness of the system. The university institutions were, therefore, requested to indicate whether they were satisfied with the state governments' efficiency in the assessment, sanction and release of state grants. The responses of the institutions reveal that only 36 per cent of the collegiate institutions and 24 per cent of the universities vouched for the satisfactory character of the present arrangements about the assessment/sanctioning of the state grants. About 51 per cent of the institutions testified to the delay in the assessment, sanction and release of state grants.

Procedural bottlenecks

The following is a summary of the procedural and other bottlenecks mentioned by most of the institutions:

(i) there is inordinate delay in the release of grants. Generally, there is duality of control; the education department assessing the grants and the finance department actually releasing it. The procedures are cumbersome and dilatory. Too many formalities have to be undergone before the grant is released. In a number of cases, the institutions complained that the release of grants was effected at the fag end of the year with the result that the institutions found it difficult to spend the grants released in a rational and fruitful manner.

(ii) institutions in a number of states complained about the period of probation, ranging from one to five years, which should elapse after the establishment of the institution, before they become eligible for state grants. One institution in Orissa remarked that the period of waiting before the institutions become eligible for state grant was like asking a 'baby to live for five years before feeding it'.

(iii) mention was also made of the 'leisurely audit', 'aweful bureaucracy', 'red tape', and so on. The need for communicating to the institutions about the items for which grants were disallowed was stressed.

Respecting academic freedom

The importance of the state governments respecting the academic freedom of the institutions, notwithstanding their being the beneficiaries of state munificence, cannot be overemphasized. The principals of colleges in three states mentioned above were requested to give their reactions to some specific aspects of academic freedom in relation to state grant-in-aid system. Their responses are summarised in Table 4.3.

It would appear that a large majority of principals have registered their complaint about states' interference in appointing teaching staff and determining courses of study. Even in the case of selecting students, some interference from the state government regulations has been mentioned.

The principals were also asked to mention a few instances of the manner in which the state regulations infringe upon the academic freedom. The typical responses are listed below:

1. No staff can be appointed without the state government's permission. In some cases, staff is selected subject to communal reservations.
2. Governments' permission is required for introducing new courses of study. The courses are decided by Director of Education/University.
3. Evaluation of students is done by the university.
4. Selection of students has to be done according to government rules. In some cases it is subject to communal reservations.

TABLE 4.3 : **Extent of academic freedom in colleges**

Constituents of academic freedom	Principals responding (Figures in percentages)	
	In favour	Against
Appointing teaching staff	31	69
Selecting students	44	56
Determining courses of study	25	75
Evaluating students' performance	50	50

To conclude

The system of grant-in-aid introduced by the different state governments needs to be rationalised and streamlined in order to make it an effective instrument of maintaining university institutions and bringing about the desired changes in the system of higher education. It must be understood that the provision of financial assistance from the state governments as also the central agencies to university institutions is not an act of benevolence grudgingly undertaken by an indifferent bureaucracy. It is an essential pre-requisite for socio-economic development in that it helps in the flowering of the intellect of the young men and women, who come under the charge of these institutions at the most formative stage of their lives. From that point of view, the grant-in-aid system should not only provide the much needed assistance to the educational institutions, but should also have the potentiality to direct the development of university institutions into desired channels.

The plea for rationalisation of the grant-in-aid system should not, however, be construed as an excuse for bringing about a morbid uniformity. Indian States have diverse problems of educational development and no single formula can be effective in all cases. The systems of grant-in-aid introduced by different states are the resultant of the varying socio-economic factors peculiar to those states. It is, therefore, necessary that without resorting to a strait-jacket approach to the financing of higher education, we should try to rid the system of grant-in-aid of its angularities and idiocyncracies, some of which have been highlighted in the preceding discussion.

ANNEXURE

SUMMARY STATEMENT GIVING PATTERNS OF GRANTS IN DIFFERENT STATES

Colleges of General Education

Maintenance grants

States meeting percentage of net deficit expenditure

100%	70-95%	Below 50%	No fixed percentage
Andhra Pradesh Assam Jammu & Kashmir Madhya Pradesh West Bengal (for Government approved colleges).	Tamil Nadu Tripura Rajasthan* Punjab	West Bengal (50% of the deficit or Rs. 30,000 whichever is less)	Haryana Bihar Himachal Pradesh Nagaland

Pay Packet

Gujarat
Karnataka
Kerala
Uttar Pradesh
Orissa (From the year, the colleges are entitled to full net deficit grant).
Maharashtra
Andhra Pradesh: When the management fails to pay salary to the teachers for two months, the Government may order direct payment to the staff (after an enquiry) from the grant payable to management.

*Grants range from 50 per cent of the net deficit to 80 per cent for category A to D colleges. Special category: 90 per cent.

Colleges of General Education

Buildings/Hostels

State meeting percentage expenditure:

50% and below	50-75%
Madhya Pradesh 1/3 in towns with a population of 10,000 or more and 50% with a population of 10,000 or less and girls' institutions. *Maharashtra* (25%) *Andhra Pradesh* First grade colleges—50% subject to a maximum of Rs. 75,000. Second grade colleges—50% subject to a maximum of Rs. 50,000. *Orissa* 50% of the estimated cost for arts colleges; $66\frac{2}{3}\%$ for science colleges. *Rajasthan* *Tamil Nadu* (Subject to a maximum of Rs. 75,000 to first grade colleges and Rs. 50,000 to second grade colleges.) *Tripura* (maximum Rs. 2 lakhs). *U.P.* (as matching share of U.G.C. grant).	*West Bengal* Men's colleges: equal to amount contributed from private sources and double the amount for women's colleges.

Colleges of General Education

States meeting percentage expenditure

Development Grants		Other Grants
50% and below	50-100%	
Gujarat	*Andhra Pradesh* (Maximum, Rs. 10,000) *Maharashtra* Rs. 30 per science student. *Rajasthan* *Tamil Nadu* (subject to a maximum of Rs. 10,000) *Tripura* *Madhya Pradesh* *Uttar Pradesh*	*Andhra Pradesh* gives ad-hoc grants to colleges in backward areas, women's colleges and colleges in rural areas. *Gujarat* gives performance grants: first three colleges will be given performance grants @ Rs. 1,00,000, Rs. 75,000 and Rs. 50,000 respectively.

(*Continued*)

Punjab

(i) Managements have to provide 1-1/2 times the amount given by the Government for equipment.

(ii) Colleges for women and in rural areas get a special grant of Rs. 3,000 each.

Rajasthan gives 25 per cent grant for a bus.

Tripura contigent grant: 90 per cent of the actual expenditure subject to 1/6 of the expenditure on staff salaries.

Haryana

1. Rs. 3,000 for women's colleges and those in rural areas.
2. Ad hoc grant up to Rs. one lakh for women's colleges and Rs. 50,000 for men's colleges and co-educational institutions.

Orissa: 80 per cent of the DA for teaching staff.

Himachal Pradesh: 100 per cent grant for revision of pay scales.

Kerala: Grants for libraries, laboratories etc. to be calculated on the per capita basis.

Orissa: Recurring grants @ Rs. 22 per student in arts and commerce colleges and Rs. 55 per student in science colleges subject to the college being qualified to receive full deficit grant.

Colleges of Technical Education

Maintenance grant

States meeting percentage of net deficit expenditure

50-75 per cent	75-100 per cent	Not specified
Andhra Pradesh (boys' polytechnics 65%).	Andhra pradesh: girls' polytechnics (80%)	Assam
	Gujarat (90%)	Bihar
	Haryna (90%)	Himachal Pradesh
	Jammu & Kashmir (100%)	Nagaland
	Karnataka (85%)	Orissa
	Maharashtra (90% of the approved expenditure.	Rajasthan
	Punjab: Degree colleges (75%) diploma (90%)	Madhya Pradesh
	Tamil Nadu (90%)	
	West Bengal 100% of the deficit.	
	Direct payment of salary	
	Kerala	
	Uttar Pradesh,	

Colleges of Technical Education

Building grants

States meeting percentage expenditure

Below 50 per cent	50 per cent and above
Andhra Pradesh (boys 25%, girls 12-1/2%)	Karnataka (Subject to a maximum of Rs. 50,000 per annum).
Haryana (varying proportions)	Tamil Nadu: 90 per cent (within the ceilings fixed by the Southern Regional Committee of the All India Council for Technical Education).
Kerala (25%)	
Madhya Pradesh (up to Rs. 5 lakhs)	

5

FEDERAL GRANTS

BEFORE the 42nd amendment of the Constitution, which placed education as a whole in the concurrent list of the Seventh Schedule of India's Constitution, 'education including universities' was a State subject. The federal government was responsible for a few central institutions besides having the obligation of looking after the coordination and determination of standards of higher education and research. In spite of this drastic structural change in the Indian Constitution, the Central government has, so far, given no indication of exercising its extended powers under the amended Constitutional framework. The federal government's policy of non-interference in the educational prerogatives of the state governments can be easily discerned by its unwillingness to curb the enthusiasm of the state governments to set up universities and colleges primarily to serve socio-political interests rather than to satisfy assessed academic requirements.

The position is somewhat complicated by the fact that the federal government itself is a centrifugal entity. Although the concept of joint responsibility of the cabinet is the sheet-anchor of the parliamentary system of government, from the very nature of things, the administration and financing of higher education vest in various ministries with little coordination among them.

The departmental heterogeneity at the federal level is reflected in the multiplicity of specialised bodies to fulfil the central responsibility in the field of higher education. The important organisations include the University Grants Commission, the Indian Council of Agricultural Research, the Indian Council of Social Science Research and the Indian Council of Medical Research and so on. These bodies are concerned with the financing of the institutions relating to their respective disciplines as also providing them academic guidance consistent with their role of coordination of standards. All these organisations have laid down rules and regulations governing financial assistance to their respective institutions.

The most prominent among these organisations is the University Grants Commission, which was established through an Act of Parliament in 1956. During over two and a half decades of its existence, the Commission has given financial assistance to the universities and colleges for various development programmes ranging from trivial items like the setting up of chalk boards, shooting ranges and so on to the prestigious programmes like the development of post-graduate departments, promotion of research facilities and the setting up of centres of advanced studies and autonomous colleges.

The Indian Council of Agricultural Research is functioning more or less on the lines of the UGC with its operational activities limited to agricultural universities and colleges. The Council has provided assistance for the development and maintenance of agricultural universities. Besides, it also assists agricultural colleges for their development. The ICAR's assistance is available for college buildings, equipment, library, workshop, student hostels, staff quarters, sports and games and so on.

The ICSSR is mainly concerned with the promotion of research in social sciences. The Council provides financial assistance for research projects, besides awarding research fellowships and giving publication grants. The Council has so far assisted 708 research projects and given 323 fellowships.[1]

The Indian Council of Medical Research, the Indian Council of Historical Research, the National Council of Educational Research and Training and a number of government departments provide assistance mainly for the promotion of research activities in their respective disciplines. While the procedures of grants adopted by these bodies have been examined in a subsequent chapter, it is considered appropriate to examine the procedures of assistance by the UGC which, as already stated, is the premier grant giving body set up by the central government.

POLICY FRAMEWORK

The UGC has delineated the policy framework for the development of higher education in India over the next 10 to 15 years. The policy frame aims at a drastic overhaul of the educational system through the inculcation of a modern scientific outlook. It emphasises programmes of adult education and the introduction of universal elementary education. Secondary education is to be terminal in character and vocationalisation will permeate the entire educational system.

In regard to higher education, the policy frame repeats the guidelines that have been emphasised time and again by various commissions and committees. To mention a few :

(i) adoption of measures which will reduce pressure on the university system such as effective vocationalisation at the secondary stage, delinking most of the jobs from degrees, and changing the present recruitment policies which virtually make a degree a minimum qualification for any good job;

(ii) exercising great restraint in the establishment of new institutions, which should not be set up (except in backward areas) unless their need is clearly established on sound academic considerations and adequate resources in terms of men, materials and money are available;

(iii) planning the location of new institutions very carefully and rationalising the existing ones to the extent possible;

(iv) adopting a policy of selective admissions to full-time institutions of higher education at first degree and post-graduate levels on the basis of merit with reservation of at least half the seats for all weaker sections;

(v) enabling talented but economically weaker students to pursue their studies on a whole-time basis by ensuring to them the full cost of their education through appropriate bursaries, for which funds may be raised from public and private bodies;

(vi) providing facilities for expansion of higher education

through channels of non-formal education such as correspondence courses; and

(vii) opening board and university examinations to private candidates to encourage self-study.

Brave words ! The problem, however, is that the UGC has not worked out the mechanism of translating these guidelines into action. For example, to reduce pressure on universities, the measures suggested are effective vocationalisation at the secondary stage, delinking most of the jobs from degrees and adopting a policy of selective admissions to full-time institutions. The first two suggestions are extraneous to the university system and unless a policy decision is taken at the national level and implemented with the active cooperation of the state governments, nothing tangible is likely to happen. The third suggestion about adopting a policy of restrictive admissions (with reservation for the weaker sections to the extent of 50%) is extremely controversial and, in the present situation in the country, almost unworkable. The university degrees are not sought after for their potentiality for jobs only, they also provide some sort of waiting period for the student till he lands up on a suitable opening. Further, somehow or the other, the university degrees have acquired a (somewhat disproportionately higher degree of) social prestige, so much so that a non-degree holder is, more often than not, given a lower social status in our system.

The suggestions about putting restraints on the establishment of new institutions and planning the location of institutions carefully, howsoever laudable, appear to have been honoured more in breach than in compliance by the state governments, who are the real masters of the situation. Since the policy frame for the development of higher education was announced in 1978, 13 more universities and 511 colleges have been set up by various state governments. The fact of the matter is that so long as the craze for university degrees continues to remain unabated and the employment situation for the educated continues to deteriorate, it would be difficult to place a moratorium on the opening of new institutions.

The observations made above are not intended to belittle the importance of policy statements issued by the central agencies. It is, however, necessary to point out the essentiality of involving all the concerned organisations in this task so that the suggestions made by the central organisations do not remain mere declarations of pious intentions but become effective instruments of academic improvement.

PATTERN OF ASSISTANCE

The pattern of assistance from the UGC to colleges and universities has been varying from plan to plan. The latest pattern introduced by the UGC is as follows:

Colleges

Eligibility criteria
The eligibility criteria for assistance under this scheme is that the college should have at least four departments with a minimum of two teachers in each department and at least ten permanent teachers excluding the principal and the P.T.I. The overall student-teacher ratio should not be more than 30:1; it should have at least 300 students in degree classes and above, beyond plus two stage. The enrolment condition is relaxable to 200 in the case of women's colleges and colleges in backward/rural areas.

Schematic assistance
The UGC's assistance for colleges for their development programmes is related to their enrolment: Rs. 4 lakhs for enrolment between 300 and 600 and Rs. 5 lakhs for enrolment beyond 600 in multi-faculty colleges catering to arts, science and commerce courses. Besides special assistance is available for colleges in backward areas and those catering to the needs of economically and educationally backward communities.

The assistance is available for the construction of buildings for library, laboratories, classrooms, hostels, staff quarters, purchase of books and equipments and so on. The pattern of assistance varies from 50 per cent for construction/extension of buildings, staff quarters, and so on to 100 per cent for faculty improvement programmes, books and journals including book banks and equipment. For the development of post-graduate education, institutions are eligible for assistance for books, and equipments and setting up of workshops at the rate of 100 per cent of expenditure, subject to a maximum of Rs. 1.5 lakhs for each department in Humanities and Social Sciences and Rs. 2 lakhs for each department in science subjects. Additional staff—academic as well as technical—is also eligible for varying types of assistance. Besides, assistance is also available for College Science Improvement Programme (COSIP) and College Humanities and Social Sciences Improvement Programme (COHSSIP). The Commission also assists selected colleges to become autonomous colleges.

Universities

The UGC's assistance during the Sixth Plan is available on 100 per cent basis for essential inputs, like additional staff, books and journals and faculty improvement programmes. For staff quarters, academic buildings, teachers' hostels, workshop sheds, it is 50 per cent. Besides the UGC gives assistance at the rate of 50 per cent for men's hostels and 75 per cent for women's hostels. The assistance is also available for health centres and printing presses at the rate of 50 per cent.

Unlike the colleges, no financial ceilings have been laid down in the case of UGC's assistance to universities. The UGC has, however, suggested that assistance for different inputs should broadly conform to the following limits:

(a) Buildings	20 per cent of total allocations.
(b) Staff	20 to 25 per cent of total allocations.
(c) Equipment, books and journals	50 to 65 per cent of total allocations.

It would appear that the bulk of resources made available by the UGC are intended to build up the physical infrastructural facilities of the universities and colleges with some assistance for other quality improvement programmes. As stated by the UGC in its reply to the questionnaire issued by the Review Committee, the Commission has been "of the view that quality improvement can take place only in a certain level of physical environment and for this, assistance for buildings, appointment of staff, purchase of books, journals and scientific equipment and workshop facilities are unavoidable.[2]

It is difficult to question the validity of the reasoning advanced by the UGC for emphasising the improvement of physical facilities in its scheme of assistance. Two precautions are, however, necessary. Firstly, there is need to curb the tendency of 'over construction' as has happended in the case of some of the colleges and departments of agricultural universities.[3] Secondly, the development of human material should receive equal, if not more, emphasis along with brick, mortar and materials. In case a choice has to be made, the former, rather than the latter, should have precedence.

Without minimising the importance of the UGC's contribution to the development of university institutions, it may be stated that the system of finance evolved by the Commission as also the manner in which it has been implemented has given rise to a number of problems, some of which are quite serious in character. The important problems emerging from the operation of the UGC's programmes are discussed below.

'RESPONSIVE' CHARACTER OF UGC GRANTS

In spite of the promotional role assigned to the UGC, the nature of UGC's assistance has remained mainly *responsive* in character in that the UGC basically *reacts* to the proposals submitted by the universities and colleges. It can be argued that the assistance provided by the UGC is in relation to the pattern of assistance drawn up by the Commission and hence it is within the scheme of priorities worked out by it. The point to be noted, however, is that in the absence of an initiative by the Commission to undertake a precise assessment of the requirements of the university institutions, its role becomes secondary in character. The result is that an integrated development of higher education does not always take place.

Another feature of the 'responsive' nature of the UGC's grants is the absence of any mechanism available with the UGC to curb the enthusiasm of the concerned agencies—state governments and private bodies—to set up institutions of higher education without sufficient academic justification. The position has become somewhat complicated because of the lack of clear-cut demarcation of responsibility in higher education between the central and the state governments. Under the Constitution, the state governments can set up the universities and colleges in the hope that the UGC will, at some stage, take over the onerous task of improving their standards as a part of its constitutional responsibility.

The position has not improved in spite of a feeble attempt that has been made to make the UGC have a say in the matter of setting up of universities. Under Section 12 (f) of the UGC Act, the Commission may advise any authority, *if such advice is asked for* on the establishment of a new university or on proposals connected with the expansion of the activities of any university.[4] This clause, being of a non-mandatory character, does not go too far. It may also be stated that the amended UGC Act (1972) authorises the UGC not to give grant to a university, "which is established after the commencement of the UGC (Amendment) Act, 1972, unless the Commission has, after satisfying itself as to such matters as may be prescribed, declared such university to be fit for receiving such grant".[5] This amendment, however, is at best of a negative character in that it does not authorise the UGC to stall the opening of new universities; it only empowers it to refuse financial assistance to such institutions that have been set up without the previous concurrence of the UGC. The fact that quite a few universities were set up without the concurrence of the UGC after the amended UGC Act came into force is an eloquent testimony to the ineffectiveness of the UGC in this regard.

The position of colleges is still worse in that even the state governments do not bother much about such institutions. By and large, extra-academic considerations, rather than the assessed needs of the area, are the prime determinants in the setting up of collegiate institutions. Further, the collegiate institutions, in some states, have to wait for as long as 9 years to be eligible for state assistance. The UGC's insistence on stricter rules of affiliation has also not helped much in that 'inadequately provided colleges have been coming up here and there.[6] The only leverage available to the UGC is again declaring these institutions as non-viable institutions[7] and denying them their assistance. This, according to the UGC has, however, not been sufficient to deter the unplanned proliferation of colleges and so the problem remains as intractable as ever.[8]

It is, therefore, necessary that the UGC should adopt a promotional role in higher education. This can be done by taking initiative in assessing the requirements of various types of institutions of higher education and providing assistance on the basis of that assessment. Even in the setting up of new institutions, the UGC should provide the technical and academic guidance to the state gavernments and private bodies. If the implementation of this suggestion necessitates an amendment of the UGC' Act, that should be provided. It would also necessitate improving the UGC's capability for monitoring and assessing the educational needs of different areas and providing the necessary guidance to the states and private organisations intending to open educational institutions. The point that needs to be emphasised, even at the cost of repetition, is that the UGC should shed its policy of *laissez-faire* in matters academic and should take initiative in fulfilling its role of coordination and determination of standards of higher education and research.

SCHEMATIC PROLIFERATION

In the initial stages, the UGC was assisting the universities and colleges for a large number of schemes. The schemes included, among others, such items as improvement of chalk boards, construction of shooting ranges, water coolers, cycle sheds and so on. The list has been substantially reduced in the Sixth Plan. Even then, schemes like canteens, health centres, extension programmes and cultural activities have been retained. It is not the intention to undervalue the importance of these schemes for the all round development of university institutions. It would, however, be conceded that, in an economy of scarcity, the UGC would be well advised to restrict the area of its operation to programmes, which have a direct bearing on its constitutional responsibilities.[9] The schemes, which are of local interest, should be left to local initiative.

INEQUITOUS FINANCIAL ASSISTANCE

More serious than the floating of schemes of ephemeral character is the inequitous distribution of financial assistance. An analysis of the financial policies pursued by the UGC reveals that the UGC has been more munificent to the universities—within the universities to central universities—than to colleges, which are responsible for adout 83 per cent of the enrolment at the higher education stage. It has been reckoned that during the period 1975-76 to 1981-82, the UGC released a total amount of about Rs. 276 crores—Rs. 225 crores for the universities and Rs. 51 crores for the colleges. This works out to Rs. 643 per student per annum in the universities and a mere Rs. 29 per student in the colleges! The magnitude of the disparate treatment can be realised by the following table 5.1:

TABLE 5.1: **Financial assistance given by UGC to universities and colleges**

	Grants released by UGC		Student enrolment (in lakhs)	
	Total (Rs. crores)	Percentage to total	Total	Percentage to total
Universities	225.1	81.7	5.00	16.8
Colleges	50.5	18.3	24.03	83.2
Total	275.6	100.0	29 00	100.00

It would appear that the universities, which account for about 17 per cent of the student enrolment, were the recipient of about 82 per cent of the developmental outlays provided by the UGC during the period 1975-82. During the corresponding period, the colleges, which are responsible for about 83 per cent of the enrolment, received 18 per cent of the UGC's assistance. In the context of this comparative analysis, the following factors have to be taken into account:

(a) the UGC is fully responsible for the development and maintenance of the central universities and their colleges. It has to provide for the matching contribution which, in the case of state universities, has to be paid by the state governments.

(b) the overhead costs in the universities are much higher than those in the colleges; and

(c) a number of colleges are non-viable institutions and hence are ineligible for UGC's assistance.

State-wise variations

The data about the per student grant from the UGC for the different types of institutions in various states further substantiate the inequitous character of the Commission's grants. In 1981-82, the UGC's grants per student for colleges and universities were as given in Table 5.2.

Table 5.2 reveals disparities among the states in the allocation of grants for universities and colleges. It also brings to focus the vast differences in the quantum of assistance from the UGC for the universities and colleges. The causative factors for this phenomenon need further investigation. The intention, in this analysis, is to underline the disparate character of UGC's grants.

THE PROBLEM OF MATCHING SHARE

A number of schemes sponsored by the UGC involve a stipulated contribution by the university institutions or the state governments. This has not worked satisfactorily because, at least in the initial stages, the UGC did not consider it necessary to take the state governments, who have to make the matching contribution, into confidence. The result was that the collegiate institutions could not take up schemes requiring matching contributions. This lacuna has since been removed substantially by the UGC associating the state representatives with the visiting committees that assess the needs of the university institutions.

The basic question of the matching assistance, however, remains. The matching assistance involves not only the concurrence but also the ability and williingness of the other party—state government or the institution itself—to make the requisite contribution. They have also to undertake full

TABLE 5.2 : **States receiving per student average annual grant—1981-82**

(Figures in Rupees)

(i) Colleges

Below 10	10-20	20-30	30-40	40-50	50 & above
Gujarat	Haryana	Assam	Andhra Pradesh	Tamil Nadu	Orissa
Karnataka	Himachal Pradesh	Bihar			
Madhya Pradesh	Jammu & Kashmir	Kerala			
	Maharashtra	Uttar Pradesh			
	Punjab				
	Rajasthan				
	West Bengal				

(ii) Universities

Below 500	500-1,000	10,00-1,500	1,500-2,000	2,000 & above
Rajasthan	Bihar	Andhra Pradesh	Jammu & Kashmir	Kerala
Haryana	Gujarat	Assam	Orissa	
	Karnataka	Himachal Pradesh		
	Uttar Pradesh	Madhya Pradesh		
	West Bengal	Maharashtra		
		Punjab		
		Tamil Nadu		

responsibility for continuing the scheme after the cessation of U.G.C.'s assistance. In a number of cases, the ability and/or willingness is not available and hence the scheme fails to be implemented. As pointed out by the UGC . . . . "the utilisation of plan funds by the state universities remains inadequate or is sometimes delayed by the fact that state universities are required to give matching contribution and also assurance from the state governments regarding the maintenance of faculty positions after the assistance from the commission ceases."[10] The UGC's Standing Committee on the development of colleges expressed the same problem about the slow progress of the schemes relating to colleges.[11]

The solution of this problem would be to increase the number of schemes with 100 per cent assistance from the Commission. The Commission could select those schemes which are important from the national point of view and are in keeping with its constitutional responsibilities. These schemes could be assisted fully, without requiring any matching assistance.[12] The other schemes, which are of local interest, could be financed by the state governments/institutions. It may be mentioned that the Indian Council of Agricultural Research has also felt that "the stipulation of matching assistance was acting as a bottleneck to the development of some of the institutions and hence the ICAR proposes to do away with this during the Sixth Plan period and adopt a uniform pattern of 100 per cent assistance from the ICAR. . . ."[13]

To sum up

The federal government has been made constitutionally responsible for the coordination and determination of standards of higher education and research. To discharge this responsibility a number of federal agencies have been set up. The most important organisation set up by the federal government is the University Grants Commission, which has evolved a pattern of grant-in-aid to achieve the objectives of improving standards of higher education.

An examination of the policies and procedures evolved by the UGC for the furtherance of its objectives reveals that although considerable progress has been achieved in the realisation of these objectives, certain aspects of the procedures and policies need to be modified. The most important reform needed is to emphasise the promotional rather than the responsive role of the UGC. There is also need for making the Commission more effective in the planning of higher education, so that the proliferation of non-viable institutions, set up on extra-academic considerations, could be reduced. It is also necessary that the UGC's grants should be made more equitous. There is also need for rationalising the schemes of assistance in terms of the constitutional responsibilities of the UGC. As a corollary to this, the UGC should enlarge the area of its operation involving 100 per cent assistance.

NOTES AND REFERENCES

1. As on 31.12.1976
2. Report of the Review Committee of the UGC, 1977.
3. According to the Review Committee on Agricultural Universities (1979), surplus capacity (in some of the colleges and departments) has been constructed in a few areas without any possibility of its being used in the next fifteen or twenty years. The tendency to provide for all space requirements for each college has also led to construction of duplicate facilities in terms of class rooms, seminar rooms, etc. (See Report, p. 91).
4. UGC Act, 1956, p. 6.
5. Ibid. p. 70.
6. Report of the Review Committee of the UGC, 1977, p. 60.
7. According to UGC, 45.3 per cent of the colleges in 1979-80 were non-viable. The honour of having the highest proportion of non-viable colleges among the major states went to Assam (61%), followed by Himachal Pradesh (60%), Punjab (57%) and Orissa (56.7).
8. UGC Report for the year 1975-76, New Delhi, p. 2.
9. The Review Committee on the UGC made a reference to this aspect. According to the Committee, during the years 1966-67 to 1973-74, the UGC gave Rs. 2.8 crores for schemes which did not appear to have direct bearing on standards. (See Report of the Review Committee, op. cit., p. 60).
10. UGC Report for the year 1976-77, New Delhi, p. 102.
11. Ibid. p. 120.
12. The Review Committee of the UGC has also made the same suggestions, though for a different reason. The Committee said: . . . "... As a modification of the matching formula, it is worth considering that improvement programmes for certain sectors of edu-

cation like post-graduate education and research be assisted on 100 per cent basis so that quality improvement programmes are implemented in a uniform manner by all universities and colleges . . ." (Report of the Review Committee on the UGC, 1977, p. 6).

13. Report of the Review Committee on Agricultural Universities, Indian Council of Agricultural Research, 1978, p. 84.

6

SUPPORT FOR RESEARCH

RESEARCH in India is of a comparatively recent origin. During the later half of the nineteenth century, when universities were set up in the Presidencies of Bombay, Calcutta and Madras, the main function of these institutions was to hold examinations. Teaching and research, as functions of the universities, were added much later. In the tuwilight of the British *Raj*, however, some attention was paid to institutional research in specific areas through the setting up of research councils in science and technology and agriculture.

Research activity received a fillip during the post-independence period, which saw the establishment of a number of grant giving bodies for, among other things, promoting research in their respective disciplines. The prominent among such organisations are the University Grants Commission, the Indian Council of Social Science Research, the Indian Council of Historical Research and so on. Specialised institutions like the institutes of technology, medicine and physical and biological science were also set up for undertaking research in their specific disciplines.

The expenditure on research and development in India is, however, at a somewhat low level. In 1966, the Education Commission estimated that the current level of expenditure on research and development in India was about one rupee per capita; nearly 0.3 per cent of the G.N.P. According to the Commission, India was almost at the bottom end of the international ladder.[1]

It is heartening to note that in the recent past, considerable emphasis has been laid on research and development effort through increased financial inputs. In Table 6.1, the latest position about financial allocations on research and development in India as also some of the countries in Asia, Europe and America has been indicated. In order to make the comparison meaningful, all the expenditures have been converted into U.S. dollars.

TABLE 6.1 : **Expenditure on R & D (selected countries)**

(*in US dollars*)

Country	Year	Total expenditure (000)	As percentage of GNP	Per capita	Average annual per scientist or engineer
India	1977	4,60,415.35	0.5	0.76	16,310.55
Indonesia	1976	46,986.71	0.2	0.35	6,145.98
Republic of Korea	1981	34,934.96	0.6	9.15	18,951.41
Israel	1978	3,53,872.25	2.5	95.90	2,403 50
U S.A.	1980	62,282,500.00	2.4	273.60	97,700.00
U.K.	1978	67,38,020.80	2.2	120.74	77,931.70
U.S.S.R.	1980	28,54,200.00	4.6	107.47	20,770.00

Source : Statistical Year Book, UNESCO, 1982, Table 5.14.

There has been marked increase in the per capita expenditure on R and D in India during the post-Education Commission (1964-66) period. From rupee one per capita on research development in 1966, we have reached a somewhat respectable figure of about Rs. 8 per capita in 1977. Lest this should lead us to a false sense of complacency, it may be emphasised that : (a) The enhancement should be seen in the light of the fact that considerable erosion has taken place in the value of money since 1966, when the Education Commission reported; and (b) India compares unfavourably even among some of the countries in Asia, not to speak of the advanced countries of the world. Even the war ravaged Republic of Korea is spending twelve times more per capita on R and D than this country. We have to go a long way in order to reach the position attained by the advanced countries of the world so far as R & D effort is concerned.

INTER-REGIONAL VARIATIONS

It may also be pointed out that there are wide variations ir the research inputs and outputs in the various regions of th country. This was revealed in a study on social science researcl sponsored by the ICSSR[2] The following Table 6.2 sums ur the position:

TABLE 6.2 : **Inter-regional variations in per Institute expenditur and research output : 1974-75—1977-78**

	Eastern region	Northern region	Southern region	Western region
Average age of the institute (in years)	14.2 (4)	14.8 (3)	15.0 (2)	16.0 (2)
Per institute expenditure (Rs. in lakhs)	31.95 (4)	38.56 (3)	47.99 (2)	62.00 (1)
Projects undertaken (per institute)	12 (4)	16 (1)	13 (3)	15 (2)
Projects completed (per institute)	6 (3)	8 (1)	7 (2)	4 (4)
Books published (per institute)	14 (2)	15 (1)	8 (3)	14 (2)
Project reports published (per institute)	4 (2)	5 (1)	2 (3)	2 (3)

Note : Figures in brackets show the rank of the respective regions.

It is interesting to note that there is some sort of invers correlation between the expenditure per institute and th research output as measured by projects completed or book published. The study, however, relates to the number o projects/books and does not vouchsafe the quality of th product.

It may be admitted that for a long time to come, it woul

not be possible for this country to make adequate financial inputs for research and development. It is, therefore, imperative that maximum use may be made of the financial allocations available to different agencies concerned with sponsoring and financing of research programmes. This would necessitate a very careful assessment of the research needs of the country, laying down priority areas in research and streamlining rules and regulations governing grant-in-aid for research.

Patterns and procedures of research grants

It is proposed to examine below the patterns and procedures laid down by the various bodies concerned with funding/sponsoring research in different disciplines. The problems emerging from the operation of the grant-in-aid rules and suggestions for improving the system will also be given wherever necessary.

Programmes eligible for financial support

The programmes eligible for financial support from the different funding bodies could be grouped under the following heads:

1. Research Projects,
2. Fellowships and Scholarships, and
3. Publications.

The rules and regulations governing grants for the abovementioned programmes are reviewed below:

RESEARCH PROJECTS

Priority areas

The organisations concerned with research grants have generally laid down priority areas of research. For example, the Indian Council of Historical Research has identified preferential areas like social and economic formation processes in India, covering all periods and all parts of the country; history of material culture including science and technology; local history including surveys of source materials and antiquities found in different areas of the country; history of national movement with special reference to the role of the people, and so on.

The Indian Council of Social Science Research has stated that the Council would give higher priority to its promotional role than to its responsive role. The promotional role would be geared to selected disciplinary and inter-disciplinary programmes in general and to the objectives of the Five Year Plans in particular. Out of 15 research programmes selected for sponsorship by the ICSSR, 7 have been taken up. They are: (i) Poverty and Unemployment; (ii) Public Distribution System; (iii) Rural Development; (iv) Government System and Development; (v) Urban Studies; (vi) Area Studies; and (vii) Problems and Status of Women.

The Council of Scientific and Industrial Research has established a network of laboratories concerned with research in various scientific and technological subjects. The main areas of research are chemistry, physics, biological science and other branches of sciences.

The priority areas in research as delineated by the University Grants Commission relate to projects that have a direct relevance to the problems of the community. While drawing up research programmes having research and development, it is required that the areas identified as of R & D importance by the National Committee on Science and Technology and C.S.I.R. are kept in view.

The Indian Council of Agricultural Research has laid down areas of special thrust in research. These include, among others, Agricultural Economics—economic evaluation of new agricultural technology for specific regions; Economic priority for agrobiological research from a long-term perspective for different crops and regions; Irrigation—management, water pricing and economics of water use; Economic aspects of energy requirements; Rural poverty; Agrarian reforms; Agricultural finance and so on. The Council also sponsors and supports research projects of a long-term and short-term character.

The Department of Social Walfare of the Government of India sponsors research projects of an applied nature in the fields of social welfare, social policy and social development, keeping in view plan policies and programmes and social problems requiring urgent public attention.

The priority areas delineated by the National Council of Educational Research and Training include research and innovations which will promote the fulfilment of the Constitutional Directive or Article 45 relating to the provision of free and compulsory education for all children up to the age of 14, with particular reference to extending the educational programmes to girls and to the weaker sections of the community, specially the scheduled castes and scheduled tribes.

The priority areas laid down by the Indian Council of Medical Research coincide with the national health priorities viz. control of communicable diseases, fertility control, promotion of maternal and child health, control of nutritional and major metabolic disorders, developing alternative strategies for health and delivery system through primary health care approach for the fulfilment of the goal of health for all by A.D. 2000, containment within safety limits of occupational, environmental, health burdens, selected studies in non-communicable diseases. . . . These studies are regarded as an interactive continuum rather than as competitive entities.

Conditions for grants

The various organisations have laid down almost similar conditions for research grants. The items eligible for assistance include appointment of research, technical and other staff, travel, field work, apparatus and equipment, postage, stationery, printing of questionnaires, books, journals, contingencies and similar other items. There are, however, some differences in the categories of staff and other items eligible for assistance from these organisations. For example, the Indian Council of Medical Research does not provide for non-scientific personnel like technicians, laboratory assistants, clerks, and so on. The Indian Council of Agricultural Research does not normally provide for the supporting personnel such as field/laboratory assistants or helpers, clerks, typists, and so on, except in exceptional circumstances in the interests of project work. The Indian Council of Social Science Research, the Council of Historical Research, the National Council of Educational Research and Training, however, provides for full complement of staff of various categories, subject to the maximum of consolidated remuneration prescribed by these organisations.

Almost all the organisations do not allow any salary for

the project director who, according to them, should be honorary.[3] This provision may, at times, prove to be a handicap in the furtherance of research because no researcher, who is unemployed, will agree to work honorarily regardless of his competence to take up that work. In case he is employed, he would have very little time to devote himself to the work of the project. In both these situations, the progress of the project will be retarded. It is, therefore, advisable that the project director should normally be a full-time employee, and should devote himself entirely to research work. In case an employed academic wants to take up research work, the Council should, while considering his proposal, take into consideration the workload that he has already on hand and decide about his association in the light of that study.

Fellowships

Different central organisations have initiated schemes of fellowships for, among other things, doctoral and post-doctoral research. At the apex is the scheme of national fellowships, which is given to outstanding scholars in the universities and non-university organisations for full-time study and research, free from their normal teaching and other administrative responsibilities. The scheme entitles the scholar to draw salary and allowances as also an annual amount for contingencies. In actual operation, however, the scheme has tended to be more of a recognition of the intellectual eminence of the scholar rather than a goal-oriented academic endeavour.

While it is difficult to deny the desirability of honouring the best brains of the country, the form of recognition could be somewhat different. As suggested by the Second Review Committee of the ICSSR, the Council could "offer to bring together and publish the collected works of scholars. Or the ICSSR may arrange to bring out a volume of essays in his honour, contributed by senior social scientists.[4]" The Committee went on to say:

> We believe that the fellowships must have a quid pro quo and, therefore, while offering the national fellowships, the ICSSR should make it clear that a substantial work is ex-

pected and evolve a modus operandi, whereby the progress is periodically reported.[5]

Senior fellowships

The basic idea of senior fellowships is to enable scholars to undertake whole-time research by *buying* their time from other responsibilities. The fellowship does not carry any financial incentives but protects the actual salary and other benefits available to the scholars. The fellowship is tenable for a period of two years, extendable to third year in exceptional cases. The fellow is entitled to an annual contingent grant of varying amounts under the rules framed by different organisations. The UGC is also operating a number of schemes for encouraging the outstanding teachers in universities and colleges to undertake research.

The scheme of senior fellowships has not been very popular. For example, the ICSSR had hoped that about 20 fellowships will be awarded each year. Against this, the average annual intake has been mere 11! This is mainly because of the following reasons:

(i) Most of the universities have tedious procedures for study leave. It also involves loss of increments when a teacher goes on such a fellowship. The contingency grant is also inadequate to meet the research costs. The absence of adequate research assistance also often proves to be a serious handicap.

(ii) there are some structural problems as well. The tradition of such fellowship is not sufficiently developed in the country. Nor are there many institutions, which encourage outside scholars to work with them, so that academic community could benefit from such exchanges. Housing, in most of the institutions, is also difficult.

(iii) there are disparities in the amount of scholarships and fellowships offered by central agencies. In view of this, the UGC has suggested that the scholarships and fellowships awarded by different organisations to candidates of comparable qualifications should not vary widely as regards their value and the conditions of award. It would be of advantage if the various schemes for the award of scholarship and fellowships could be coordinated by some central agency. . . .[6]

So far as the procedural and practical problems concerning these fellowships are concerned, it is suggested that the matter may be discussed with the University Grants Commission and the universities in order to evolve a procedure of expeditious relieving of persons selected for the senior fellowships. Further, sufficient incentives should be given to the fellows to work on projects of their choice.

Publication grants

The escalating costs of printing and the tendency on the part of the publishers to make a fast buck have thrown the publication of the works of learned nature out of gear. The fact that the commercial value of such works is in inverse proportion to the profundity of thought encompassed therein has tended to militate against the publication of such scholarly works. There is, therefore, need for publication grants by the Governmental agencies if only to enable the flame of research and scholarship to continue to illuminate the dark and dingy holes of ignorance and superstition.

It may be noted that the various organisations are not giving sufficient priority to publications of works of scholarly nature. The ICSSR had all but suspended the scheme. This has been recently revived but the coverage is extremely limited. For example, in 1981-82, only two theses and two research reports were considered eligible for the award of publication grants. The UGC has also been giving lesser emphasis to this scheme. In 1979-80, the Commission gave Rs. 9.33 lakhs as publication grant to universities and colleges. This was reduced to Rs. 8.9 lakhs in 1981-82. The inadequacy of these grants can be realised by the fact that on an average, they work out to Rs. 7,000 per university and about Rs. 10 per college per annum.

The inadequacy of grants for publication has come in for critical comments by the Review Committee on UGC's programmes (1981). The Committee said: "While we endorse the objectives of the scheme of publication of theses and learned works, it seems that they have not been achieved fully. It has come to our notice that a number of learned works remained unpublished."[7] There is, therefore, need for giving due emphasis to the publications/programmes sponsored by various agencies.

An analytical review

The preceding analysis of the rules and regulations governing financial support for research has brought to focus some of the procedural and operational problems concerning the various research programmes. These problems are not intractable and it should not be beyond the ingenuity of those concerned with financing the research programmes to solve them. In the preceding paragraphs, some suggestions have also been made to remove the lacunae observed in the grant-in-aid system. There are, however, certain more fundamental issues concerning the functioning of the research funding bodies and the implementation of the grant-in-aid schemes. A brief discussion of these problems follows.

Overlapping functions

A study of the areas of research and the priorities evolved by various organisations shows considerable overlap in their functions. The University Grants Commission, which is statutorily responsible for the coordination and determination of standards of higher education and research has been assisting research programmes in various disciplines including social and physical sciences. The Indian Council of Social Science Research, which also has been set up by the central government to promote research in social sciences, has delineated almost the same disciplines as assisted by the UGC. The Indian Council of Historical Research has been constituted to assist programmes of research in history and allied subjects. The National Council of Educational Research and Training has taken up programmes of assistance for research and education, which again figures in the respective responsibilities of the organisations like the UGC and the ICSSR. The Council of Scientific and Industrial Research has also ambitious programme of research in physical and biological sciences.

There is no mechanism available to these organisations for coordinating their activities, except through informal discussions. It would be beyond the purview of this analysis to question the appropriateness of setting up a number of organisations with almost similar or overlapping functions. It is, however, desirable to evolve a suitable machinery for coordination of activities undertaken by these organisations. The need for such coordination was realised by the Second Review Committee of the ICSSR, which recommended:

> If possible, the ICSSR may periodically appoint committees to review the research proposals being currently submitted not only to the ICSSR, but also to the UGC and other funding agencies and point out gaps and imbalances in the current research. They may indicate what in their opinion should be the priorities. More importantly, they may outline the scope of appropriate research methods for each theme so identified. This is a service badly needed by the vast majority of social science teachers, who must be drawn into the research activities.[8]

Passive role

It has been observed that in spite of the fact that the funding organisations have delineated priority areas in research, their role mainly consists of *reacting* to specific proposals made by individual researchers and institutions. This attitude of passive acquiescence needs to be changed to a more active participation in promoting research activities. The funding bodies should not only provide funds for research projects submitted to them but should also formulate projects, keeping in view their scheme of priorities; and get them investigated through appropriate institutions and individuals. In this context, mention may be made of the studies on university finances sponsored by the ICSSR. The Planning Commission also sponsors certain specific studies particularly through the Programme Evaluation Organisation. These examples need to be multiplied.

The funding bodies may also organise seminars and workshops on inter-disciplinary research themes with a view to giving an opportunity to potential researchers to contribute papers on subjects of their choice and to familiarise themselves with the latest thinking on the various subjects. These seminars should be supplemented by courses in research methodology, so as to equip the teachers and others desirous of undertaking research to improve their academic and professional competence.

Institutional concentration

It has been observed that partly because of the location of almost all the funding bodies in a particular region of the country and partly because of easy accessibility of certain institutions to the corridors of power, a large bulk of the research projects tend to be concentrated in a few institutions. This 'intellectual monopolisation' has been brought to focus by a number of committees appointed from time to time. For example, the Second Review Committee of the ICSSR gave the following details about the projects financed by the Council:

> Out of the 708 research projects financed by the ICSSR between 1969 and 1977, almost 600 have gone to the established university departments and research institutions and barely 56 to teachers in affiliated colleges. Nearly a quarter of the research projects are located in Delhi. It is true that the university training of a large majority of social science teachers in affiliated colleges and of many in a number of university departments and even of research institutes is not adequate for them to undertake research. It will be unrealistic and unfair to the ICSSR not to recognise this fact. But at the same time, to let this majority remain outside the mainstream of the social science research is undesirable and will undoubtedly prove detrimental to the development of social sciences in the country. The ICSSR must wake up to this danger.[9]

The position of the award of fellowships is no different. The First Review Committee of the ICSSR (1973) lamented that 'of the 50 fellowship awards reported in the ICSSR Newsletter of February 1973, 23 were awarded to two universities in one city and within that city, 14 out of the 23 went to one of the two universities'.[10] That the position had not changed even after the lapse of five years was highlighted by the Second Review Committee of the ICSSR, which pointed out that 'out of 323 awarded and accepted fellowships, 158 are in Delhi and that, within Delhi, as many as 106 are in the Jawaharlal Nehru University. . . ".[11]

The anomalies in the financing of the institutions by the UGC has already been alluded to. It has been pointed out that, by accident or design, the UGC has chosen to bestow its favours to certain selected institutions, while the large bulk of institutions, particularly the affiliated colleges, have been denied their legitimate share of the UGC's munificence. The latest to join the band of conscientious objectors against the skewed distribution of the UGC's funds is the Review Committee of the UGC (1977) which has given the analysis of the grants distributed by the UGC during the Fourth Plan period as shew in Table 6.3:

TABLE 6.3 : **Average development grant per institution as well as per students per annum**

Name	Per institution (figures in lakhs of rupees)	Per student (Rs.)
Central universities	88.57	1,192
State universities	12.03	337
Delhi colleges	2.90	319
Colleges of other universities	0.15*	23

*This has been calculated on the basis of total enrolment of all colleges, whether or not receiving grants from the UGC. Even after excluding the number of colleges not covered by UGC grants, the per student grant would not exceed Rs. 35 per annum and grant per college would not exceed Rs. 0.20 lakh per annum.

Source : Review Committee of the UGC, 1977, p. 57.

The disparate treatment meted out by the UGC to the central and state universities has also been commented upon by another Review Committee of UGC (1981), which stated: "A major weakness that we have noted in the implementation of programmes is regarding the uneven distribution of grants among central and state universities on the one hand and universities and colleges on the other. . .".[12]

The projects funded by the Indian Council of Agricultural

Research follow the same pattern. To quote the Review Committee on Agricultural Universities:

> Although the ICAR has located coordinated research projects strictly on technical considerations—agro-climatic suitability of a location, availability of scientists and working facilities—it so happens that some of the universities like the Punjab Agricultural University—have attracted considerably large number of ICAR projects compared to others. Therefore, there appears to be justification for reviewing the participation of agricultural universities in ICAR projects, so that the newly established universities are also given due consideration, while sanctioning new research projects or expanding the existing ones.[13]

It would be conceded that academic potentialities are not evenly distributed. It may also be admitted that an essential pre-requisite for research is the availability of academic infrastructure, which the smaller institutions may not be able to provide. It is, however, unimaginable that a large bulk of institutions are denuded of talent and are incapable of providing proper atmosphere for academic pursuits. In fact, the denial of funds for research to these institutions gives rise to a vicious circle: the institutions thus denied cannot attract talented researchers and because such persons avoid these institutions, they are denied of funds! In the interest of academic advancement, this circle needs to be broken. The point that needs to be re-emphasised is that accessibility to the decision-making authorities should not be the major determinant of eliglbility for research grants. The talent, wherever it exists, should be identified and given due recognition.

It may also be helpful to bring about some sort of decentralisation in the functioning of the central organisations. The funds for research should be placed at the disposal of the organisations located at convenient places in different regions. These organisations should work under the overall policy laid down by the central body, but should be competent to consider the proposals for research and distribute grants. These bodies should have a budget of their own and should work as the eyes and ears of the central organisations. This regional organisations should not only provide funds for research but should also have a promotional role. They should scout for talent and provide the requisite facilities for the optimisation of their research capabilities.

There is also need for wider publicity of the various schemes of different organisations for scholarships, fellowships and research grants. As it is, the universities and colleges are generally not aware of the existence of such schemes for assistance. In some cases, even the existence of the funding agencies is not known to the potential researchers. As pointed out by the Second Review Committee of the ICSSR :

> "... until now, the ICSSR assistance did not reach the social science teachers in affiliated colleges not because their research proposals were found inadequate or unsatisfactory—this might have happaned in a few cases—but because a large majority of them did not know even the existence of he ICSSR or the assistance to social science research it offers. . . . "[14]

In order to broaden the coverage of these bodies, this knowledge gap needs to be bridged.

The problem of relevance

The question of relevance of research to the socio-economic situation of the country is of utmost significance for countries of the third world, where paucity of resources in men and materials is a rule rather than an exception. It has been observed that many Indian researchers particularly in the universities have tended to ignore the question of relevance of researches in India. Somehow, the universities have assumed that their major responsibility is to encourage basic research, which is considered more in tune with their functions. On the other hand, applied research is considered more mundane in character and hence not very suitable for attention by university scholars.

It needs hardly be emphasised that there is no necessary dichotomy between basic and applied research; both are mutually complementary. As stated by the Education

Commission (1964-66) "... with the advance of science and technology, the distinction between pure and applied research—between a research scientist and a research engineer—has become artificial and in several fields (e.g. electronics) it has almost disappeared".[15] Hence, there is need for due emphasis on both pure and applied research so that the fruits of knowledge thus generated could be applied to solve the gigantic problems that the country is facing.

Lack of evaluation

There seems to be no in-built mechanism of ensuring a proper evaluation of research assistance programmes. Once a scholarship is sanctioned or a research grant is approved, it is up to the scholar to feed the sanctioning organisation with information about the progress of his work. There is no certainty that the scholar would be able to complete his project during the period envisaged in his research proposal. As a result, a number of research projects are either prolonged to the extent that they lose their relevance, or are never completed.

Problem of utilisation

The problem of utilisation of researches produced at considerable expense of finances and time also stares the researcher in the face. "The linkage between the enterprise of matching scientific research with technology of practice leading to utilisation does not operate in the area of social science with any great force in this country . . . "[16] This holds good to a certain extent, even for the physical and technological disciplines. In a number of cases, the reports of resarches do not see the light of the day. This is really frustrating to the researcher—whether individual or institutional.

To sum up

A number of organisations/agencies provide support for research in various disciplines. A few departments of the central and the state governments also provide assistance for research in the areas of their interest. While it would be unrealistic to suggest that the number of research funding agencies should be reduced to a manageable limit by merging bodies with similar functions, it is certainly necessary that overlapping in their functioning should be avoided. This could be done through the setting up of a machinery for mutual consultation at appropriate levels. These consultations should cover the question of laying down the priority areas of research, a review of the ongoing projects and the patterns and procedures of financial assistance, and so on.

The tendency to concentrate research projects in certain institutions and/or areas also needs to be curbed. While sponsoring research projects, some weightage should be given to the research proposals from the traditionally neglected institutions like the affiliated colleges and university institutions in states which are generally beyond the periphery of the perceptions of the decision making authorities. This would necessitate streamlinging the procedures of research grants, award of followships and so on. The basic consideration that should guide the funding bodies is that a few selected institutions are not necessarily the repositories of intellectual eminence. With proper encouragement, even the less developed institutions can blossom forth into reservoirs of the highest academic activity, worthy of support by these bodies.

The question of relevance of research is also of fundamental importance in countries like India, which are affilicted by a perennial inadequacy of resources. While due emphasis has to be laid on basic research, it is difficult to underrate the importane of applied research, which is directed towards solving the socio-economic problems that the country is facing.

Lastly, the utilisation of the research findings is as essential as the sponsoring of research. It is frustrating to see the research reports, so painstakingly prepared, lying unattended on the shelves of the sponsoring bodies. The sponsoring body must get the report examined and arrange for a wider dissemination of the recommendations. In case there are cogent reasons for not pursuing the findings of research report, they should be explained to the researchers.

NOTES AND REFERENCES

1. Report of the Education Commission (1964-66), New Delhi, 1966, p. 406.
2. ICSSR, *Newsletter*, October, 1980-March, 1981, p. 19.
3. The Department of Social Welfare of the Government of India, however, allows an honorarium to the project director, "after the completion of the project in case he retires from his full-time post in the middle of the project" (Grant-in-aid Rules for Research, Department of Social Welfare, New Delhi, 1976, p. 3).
4. The Second Review Committee of the ICSSR. New Delhi, 1978, p. 90.
5. Ibid., p. 90.
6. University Grants Commission, Annual Report for the year 1965-66, New Delhi, 1966, p. 46-47.
7. Review Committee on UGC Programmes, UGC, 1981, p. 36.
8. The Second Review Committee of the ICSSR, op. cit., p. 85.
9. Ibid., p. 81.
10. A Report on Social Sciences in India, Retrospective and Prospective, ICSSR, New Delhi, 1973, p. 97.
11. The Second Review Committee of the ICSSR, op. cit., p. 32.
12. Review Committee on UGC Programmes, op. cit., p. 32-34.
13. Report of the Review Committee on Agricultural Universities, ICAR, New Delhi, 1978, p, 35.
14. The Second Review Committee of the ICSSR; op. cit., p. 82.
15. Education Commission, 1964-66, op. cit., p. 413.
16. A Report on Social Sciences in India, op. cit., p. 73.

7

SOME SPECIFIC ISSUES

THE PRECEDING analysis of the system of financing of institutions of higher education has brought to focus some of the problems inherent in the system of grants from the central and the state governments. A brief analytical study of some of these problems has been made at the appropriate places. In this chapter, it is proposed to discuss in some details some of the specific issues concerning the grant-in-aid system. These problems may be grouped under the following heads :

(i) policy frame in respect of government support for higher education;
(ii) a critical examination of the patterns of grants;
(iii) resource moblisation with particular reference to :
  (a) student fees, and
  (b) private benefactions

Policy frame

In an earlier chapter, we have seen that both the federal and the state agencies concerned with the financing of higher education have laid down certain policy guidelines as also rules and regulations governing the grant-in-aid system. These rules are intended, at least theoretically, to serve the broader aims of higher education, that is, flowering of the intellect so as to widen the frontiers of knowledge. The system of socio-economic planning introduced in the country since 1951 is also meant to ensure a planned development of higher education. It was, therefore, considered necessary to study how the policies of government support for higher education are attuned to the realisation of objectives laid down in the five year plans.

In order to study this problem, we attempted to delineate the various constituents of the policy frame for the development of higher education. This delineation was based on the policy frame evolved by the U.G.C. for the sixth plan as also the objectives laid down by the Planning Commission in the sixth five-year plan. The following constituents were identified :

1. To promote qualitative improvement.
2. To provide an in-built mechanism of regulating establishment of institutions.
3. To provide for restricting student enrolment.
4. To encourage academic innovations.
5. To ensure the optimum utilisation of the existing infrastructure, before new capacities are generated, and
6. To provide incentives for restructuring curriculum.

Based on the above policy frame we attempted to ascertain the views of the principals of colleges/university authorities in the states of Andhra Pradesh, Gujarat and Haryana about the extent to which the financial and academic policies of the federal and state governments were effective in achieving these objectives.

The responses of the educational authorities in the above mentioned states are summarised in Table 7.1

It would be seen that the principals of colleges have overwhelmingly testified to the potentiality of the state/federal governments' financial policies to regulate the opening of institutions and utilising infrastructural facilities. They are almost equally divided on the question about the effectivness of the state policies to encourage academic innovations. A majority of the institutions have expressed themselves against the effectiveness of state policies to restrict student admissions or to restructure curriculum.

It is not intended to go into the causes of the ineffectiveness of the federal and state system of academic and financial management to achieve these nationally accepted objectives in higher education. There are a number of problems inherent in the implementation of these policies. For example, the

TABLE 7.1: **Principals/university authorities respondingte specific policy issues**

Percentages

Policy Issues	In Favour				Against					
	Andhra Pradesh	Gujarat	Haryana	Total	Andhra Pradesh	Gujarat	Haryana	Total	In favour	Against
Qualitative improvement	21	14	11	46	11	12	7	30	60.5	39.5
Regulating institutions	23	19	10	52	8	7	8	23	70.0	30.0
Restricting student admissions	16	9	10	35	14	17	8	39	47.3	52.7
Academic innovations	16	14	8	38	14	12	10	36	51.3	48.7
Utilising existing infrastructure	23	12	14	49	9	14	4	27	64.5	35.5
Restructuring curriculum	14	9	8	31	16	16	10	42	42.5	57.5

regulation of student admissions is an onerous task that the democratically elected governments are not in a position to achieve, in spite of their professed intentions. Similarly although promoting academic innovations is a desirable objective, it may not be supported in actual practice due to financial constraints.

In spite of the problems of finance and management involved in the implementation of the policy frame for the development of higher education, it is necessary that concerted efforts should be made to realise the nationally agreed upon objectives. Some of the constituents of the policy frame do not require large financial inputs. For example, utilising existing infrastructure and restructuring curriculum would need appropriate management techniques rather than monetary inputs. These should not be beyond the capacity of our academics and administrators. What is needed is some encouragement from the central and state authorities concerned with the financing and management of these institutions.

Patterns of grants

We shall examine below the various patterns of grants operating in different states. The most common among them are deficit grants, salary grants, block and earmarked grants, enrolment grants and so on.

Deficit grants

As has been pointed out, the grant-in-aid from the state governments is generally on the basis of deficit expenditure which, in actual fact, means approved income minus approved expenditure. The ambiguous character of the term 'approved' has already been highlighted. It has also been pointed out that even some of the essential components of expenditure have been excluded from the charmed circle of items falling within the penumbra of approbation of the state authorities.

Even if the list of approved items is updated and essential items are included, the basic question as to what extent the system of deficit grants is suitable for the university institutions remains. It was, therefore, decided to obtain the views of the institutions and experts who have had experience of the operation of the system of deficit grants from other side of the fence that is, as recipients of grants.

A perusal of the responses from 180 institutions (including 11 experts) shows that only about 39 per cent of the institutions favoured the continuance of the system. In three states, Bihar Madhya Pradesh and Uttar Pradesh, more than 50 per cent of the institutions recommended the continuance of the system. The overwhelming majority of the institutions in Andhra Pradesh rejected the system.

The typical defects of the system, as pointed out by the institutions, are :

(a) It is arbitrary and it does not take all the items of expenditure as approved items. Further, the basis of deductions made on account of those items is not intimated to the institutions;
(b) It does not offer any incentive to the institution to show good results or effect efficiency in management because the grants are available on the basis of deficit and not on the basis of the academic achievement of the institutions;
(c) It encourages uneconomical spending leading to extravagant expenditure; and
(d) In most of the states, the deficit is calculated on the basis of the previous year's expenditure, which is not an appropriate guide for the purpose.

Among the suggestions for revamping the system, the following have been mentioned by the majority of institutions :

(a) Total deficit of the institutions should be met. Some institutions have suggested that at least 75 per cent of the deficit should be shared by the government;
(b) Block grants on the basis of staff/student strength may be given;
(c) All reasonable items should be included in the 'approved' expenditure; and
(d) Current year's expenditure and not that of the previous year should be taken for calculating the deficit.

Salary grants

A number of state governments have introduced a system of salary grants under which the state governments arrange to pay staff salaries to the educational institutions. The institutions have to deposit a proportion of tuition fees with the government in order to be eligible for salary grants. A number of states have arranged direct payment of salaries to teachers through the banks/government treasury.

We had requested the principals of colleges in the states of Andhra Pradesh, Gujarat and Haryana to indicate their experience of the working of the system of salary grants. A large majority of principals have expressed satisfaction with the working of this system. The typical responses of the principals in these states are summarised below :

1. allocation order by the government is sometimes delayed.
2. grants should be given to colleges so that payment could be made in time.
3. arrear payments are delayed considerably because it requires special sanction of the education department.

Obviously, the problems mentioned by the principals are of a minor nature and can be solved by appropriate administrative action.

Block vs. earmarked grants

The grants available to the universities at present are 'block' grants, which they are entitled to receive annually from the state governments. They are free to spend the block grants to suit their needs. The 'earmarked' grants, by their very nature, are for specific projects and the universities are eligible for them only if they implement these projects.

The universities were requested to indicate their preference for block or earmarked grants. An overwhelming majority (88%) preferred the system of block grants.

Among the reasons, adduced by the universities for supporting the system of block grants, the following may be mentioned as the typical reasons:

(i) they are flexible;
(ii) they facilitate advanced planning of expenditure;
(iii) they give freedom to the institutions to experiment and, if necessary, to alter the priorities;
(iv) they are non-lapsable; and
(v) they accord with the academic autonomy of the university institutions.

In spite of the overwhelming support given to the system of block grants by the university and collegiate institutions, the system of earmarked grants is not wholly devoid of merits. An important objective of assistance to university institutions from the central and the state governments is to ensure that the broad national policies in education are kept in view by these institutions. This objective can be realised only if the grant giving authorities lay down specific goals to be achieved through a system of financial assistance. For example, if on the basis of manpower studies the state feels that the expansion of education in some particular disciplines, say, medicine or engineering or commerce, is called for, it can introduce a scheme of grants under which the universities/colleges expanding their facilities in these disciplines would be given additional financial assistance. Contrariwise, if the state feels that facilities in certain disciplines need to be curtailed, a scheme involving disincentives to the university institutions can be introduced.

The argument that the earmarked grants may infringe upon the closely guarded autonomy of the university institutions is untenable. The autonomy of the university is not an end in itself; it is a means for the efficient functioning of the institutions. If the autonomy of the institution retards the achievement of the broad national objectives of human development, which is the primary function of the institutions, the curtailment of that autonomy would be in the best interests of the country. As part of the socio-economic system, the university institutions cannot claim immunity from making constructive contribution to the realisation of national goals. As suggested by the Education Commission (1964-66), "while the universities must have the autonomy (in relation to outside agencies), it should be interpreted in the larger context of their responsibility to the nation and to mankind as a whole. . . . It is apparent that the conduct of university affairs cannot be left solely to the academics. . . ."[1]

The solution that commends itself is that while the maintenance expenditure should be given as block grants (with suitable yearly additions keeping in view the rising costs), the development grants should be given as earmarked grants. This would ensure a smooth functioning of the university institutions as also help in implementing the policies in education evolved through national consensus from time to time.

Incentive grants

A perusal of the types and quantum of state grant-in-aid, as given in the appendices, indicates that only the followlng states allow grants, which could be considered to have some semblance of the element of any incentive:

(a) Rajasthan allows higher grants for experimental institutions;

(b) Jammu and Kashmir state gives block grants for quantitative and qualitative aspects of education based on general teaching conditions, and the performance in university examination;

(c) Punjab allows special grants for women's colleges and colleges in rural areas;

(d) Gujarat state allows performance grants to three best colleges in each of the eight categories into which all the colleges in the state have been divided. The performance grants are of the value of Rs. 1 lakh for the best college and Rs. 75,000 and Rs. 50,000 each for the colleges in second and third categories. The performance is to be judged by a committee; the basis of selection being examination results, performance in extra-curricular activities and so on.

No other state has any system of incentive grants. The institutions were, therefore, requested to give their views about the desirability of such grants as also suggestions for judging the eligibility for such grants.

An analysis of the state-wise position of the institutions favouring the introduction of a system of incentive grants has revealed that a large majority of the institutions (75%) favoured the proposal. Fifty two per cent of the universities also endorsed it. The proportion of the institutions favouring the proposal has been summarised below:

State-wise percentage of institutions favouring the system of incentive grants

No response	Below 50%	50-75%	76-100%
Jammu and Kashmir	Nil	Andhra Pradesh	Assam
		Gujarat	Bihar
		Haryana	Kerala
		Karnataka	Rajasthan
		Madhya Pradesh	Tamil Nadu
		Maharashtra	Uttar Pradesh
		Orissa	West Bengal
		Punjab	

Eligibility for incentive grants

The institutions were requested to indicate the weightage that should be given to academic performance and/or distinction in co-curricular activities, while considering the eligibility of institutions for incentive grants. The analysis of institution's responses reveals that about 55 percent of the institutions favour the linking of state assistance with academic achievement. The corresponding percentage of the institutions favouring the linkage with co-curricular activities is, however, only 47.2. The percentage of universities favouring this linkage is only 32 in respect of both the proposals.

Criteria for grading institutions

The responses of the institutions about the criteria for grading the institutions for incentive grants may be summed up as follows:

(a) A large majority of the institutions, that have favoured the linkage, have suggested that it should be based on the achievement in the university examinations. This could be assessed on the basis of the percentage of students passing the various university examinations and the number of students achieving first class;

(b) About achievements in co-curricular activities, the performance in sports as observed from inter-varsity/college meets has been considered as the best criterion for grading institutions. One institution has suggested that discipline among the students may be considered as a desirable criterion;

(c) Among the other considerations, emphasis has been laid on debates and competitions, extension services, national cadet corps, national service scheme, quality of research and guidance, publications/research work by the staff, social work and community services, and so on. One university has insisted upon the maintenance of discipline and the absence of any closure of the institutions, on account of student unrest, as an important desideratum.

Regardless of what criterion is used to grade the institu-ons, the fact remains that while the basic minimum assis-ance from the state should be provided to all institutions, iere should be some incentives for those institutions, who iow consistently good performance in academic and/or co-urricular activities. Giving the same type of grants to all istitutions, regardless of their performance, would curb the nthusiasm of the institutions with potentiality for good per-ormance in curricular and co-curricular activities.

nrolment grants

t present student enrolment does not *directly* determine the uantum of state grants. It is, however, a factor to be reckon-d with while computing the eligibility of the institutions for overnment and U.G.C. assistance. Some states have also itroduced varying patterns of grants consistent with the size of udent enrolments. The general pattern of assistance, however, ontinues to be the 'deficit' system, that is, a proportion of the icome minus expenditure is provided by the state overnments.

The deficit grant system has, however, a number of draw-acks which have been pointed out earlier. There is, therefore, eed for rationalising the system of deficit grants.

The defects of the deficit system of grants can be removed

by making student enrolment as the focal point for the grant in-aid system to collegiate institutions.

The enrolment in an institution is a specific identifiabl entity. It is also possible to forecast the enrolment for th next few years with a fair degree of accuracy taking into viev the trends of admissions in the past few years, the number o students in the educational catchment area and the observe transfer ratios from secondary to university stages. Accoun may also be taken of the peculiar needs of the economy fo particular categories of manpower.

The enrolment grant formula would, however, necessitat making accurate calculations of unit costs per student a different stages of education and in different disciplines. Thes cost estimates would need to be revised periodically in relatio to the changes in the teachers' salaries and the expenditure o educational infrastructure.

Loan finance scheme

A problem that is relevant to the financing of higher educatio is whether the assistance to institutions should be in the forr of outright grants or loans. Further, whether the grant o loan should be given to the institutions or to students. In thi context it has been proposed that a larger share of public fund should be allocated directly to students as loans and the should be made to pay the full cost of their education. Th students should repay the loans without interest "after the obtain the earning stage in instalments spread over averag earning span of their life".[2]

It would be conceded that the present system of costing c higher education is somewhat inequitous in that the levels o tuition fees do not bear any relationship with the costs i institutions of higher education as well as the future earning of the university students. "The balance of argument is, there fore, in favour of bringing about a closer alignment betwee the costs of education and price students pay in the form c fees".[3] It is claimed that the loan finance scheme will remed the situation to a considerable extent.

In spite of its apparent innocuousness, the proposal i likely to give rise to quite a few conceptual and operationa problems. These include the fear that it will deter the poo students from going in for higher education because the poor families may be discouraged from undertaking a huge financial commitment. The spectre of repayment of the loan will haunt the students throughout their working life span. In the case of girls, it would be a kind of negative dowry. And what if they do not propose to work after marriage!

We think that there are two vital factors that may seriously limit the operationality of the scheme. The first is the growing unemployment and underemployment of the university educated in India. The repayment can be assured only if the university graduates and post-graduates are easily absorbed in jobs commensurate with their educational qualifications. In the absence of such a possibility, the implementation of the scheme will be severely retarded.

The second factor that may restrict its applicability is the near impossibility of operating it on an all-India scale. The experience of the scheme of national loan scholarships launched by the Ministry of Education is a clear indication of the difficulties inherent in the implementation of such schemes. The delays that occur in reaching the loan amounts to the university students and the administrative problems in recovering the loans are also to be reckoned with.

It would be prudent to implement it on an experimental basis in professional subjects like engineering and medicine, where the chances of getting employment are brighter than in other disciplines and where the future earnings of the university graduates will bear some relationship to the amount to be repaid to the government. The scheme could be extended to cover graduates with other disciplines after sufficient experience has been gained.

Resource mobilisation

We have already referred to the gradual enhancements in the proportionate contributions from the federal and state governments to college and university finances. The fee income has remained almost static and the contribution from private sources has suffered a perceptible decline. In the present state of economy, it is difficult to expect the federal and the state governments to go on increasing their contribution indefinitely. It is, therefore, necessary that efforts should be made to mobilise resources from other than the government agencies. The two main avenues open to the university institutions are student fees, and private philanthropy. There are, however, problems galore in tapping these sources. The question, therefore, merits a closer examination.

Student fees

Regardless of the complexion of the state and central grants to universities and colleges, the one single source that contributes sizeable, though proportionately declining, amounts to institutional revenues is the tuition fees paid by the students (or parents). The policy relating to fees, therefore, merits a detailed discussion. The question has assumed added significance because of the substantial decline in the proportionate contribution from philanthropic sources in the post-independence period.

POLICIES IN OTHER COUNTRIES

Before examining the Indian situation, a brief analysis of the dominant policies in other countries may be of value. In the United Kingdom, the fee contribution to university expenditure accounted for only 8 per cent of the total, an amount which according to the recommendations of the Robbins Committee was to be increased to 20 per cent. In Canada, the fee contribution was as high as 27.3 per cent of the operating incomes of the universities in 1963-64. In Sri Lanka, the students are charged no tuition fees. In West Germany, the fee contribution meets only 5 per cent of expenditure "and many students are exempted from fees including those who receive scholarships". In East Germany, tuition is free. In Australia, fees contribute only 15 per cent to expenditure on higher education. Higher education is entirely free or almost free in Afghanistan, Algeria, Argentina, Brazil, Denmark, France, Iran, Iraq, New Zealand, Norway, Poland, Turkey, U.S.S.R. and Yugoslavia. In Indonesia, the state institutions do charge fees, but they are nominal charges only. In the U.S.A., private institutions obtain a substantial part of their income from students' fees.[4]

Two conclusions can be drawn from the above analysis.

(a) Fee policies adopted in other countries are extremely diverse and offer little guidance in the development of a realistic fee policy for India, and

(b) The relative contribution from fees in India does not compare unfavourably with that in a number of advanced and developing countries. Rather, the tendency in most countries of the world is to keep the fee contribution at a low level. There is, however, one basic difference between India and most other countries. In India, because of social and democratic pressures and the non-availability of employment to a large body of post-secondary students, higher education of some form is available to almost all aspirants. By contrast, in most other countries, a policy of some selectivity in university admissions is in operation. Given the current financial conditions of stringency, no Indian Government can afford to provide high quality education to an ever-growing number of students, over whose selection it has no control. In this context, a consideration of the extent to which the students can bear an increased share of the financial burden becomes relevant.

The case for raising tuition fees

(i) The main argument in favour of raising tuition fees is that such a policy would increase the financial leverage of university and college administrators, who are often hampered in their work by a continuous depletion of resources. Harris, one of the most vocal exponents of higher tuition fees in the U.S.A., believes that even the U.S. public exchequer would be unable to meet the increasing costs of higher education without substantial support from students and parents The situation in India is much more critical and calls for quick remedial action if a total collapse of the university system is to be avoided.

(ii) The present system of low tuition fees in India amounts to a substantial subsidy for higher education. It has been reckoned that out of an average annual recurrent expenditure per student in Indian universities in 1976-77 of Rs. 3,663, only Rs. 444 (12.2%) was provided by student fees. If the non-recurrent expenditure per student is also considered, the fee contribution would then fall to about 10 per cent. Since this subsidy is given indiscriminately to rich and poor alike (the largest number of beneficiaries are from the more affluent classes, who can easily afford to provide higher education for their children), the system is, to say the least, inequitable.

(iii) Low tuition fees are inconsistent with the "open door" policy in higher education adopted by Indian universities. An increase in tuition fees would reduce the scramble for places in higher education, a demand which is often unrelated to students' capacity to benefit from such education. The resulting reduction in demand would enable the state governments to utilise their financial resources to improve the quality of education rather than to expand the institutions in order to accommodate ever-rising enrolments.

(iv) Even if one concedes that the mechanism of demand and supply cannot be the sole determinant in the pricing of the educational system, it is reasonable to expect the beneficiaries of the system to bear a reasonable part of the escalating costs. In India, there has been almost no increase in student fees during the past two decades,[5] although the wholesale price index has registered a three-fold increase. The result of this "low-cost" education has been a continuous deterioration in the quality of higher education; a situation which cannot be viewed with equanimity.

(v) College education increases substantially the earning capacity of those so educated, and if these beneficiaries were to be called upon to pay for their education, they would not be substantially worse off from such a change in policy.

The case against raising tuition fees

(i) Higher fees would provide a disincentive to poor students to continue their education at the university stage.

(ii) Education, particularly higher education, has a positive correlation with economic production, as studies by Schultz, Denison and Nallagounden have indicated, and hence society has as large a stake in the development of higher education as does the individual. In fact the social benefits of higher education far outweigh the private benefits. It would, therefore, not be legitimate to force students to contribute more than a minimal share towards the cost involved.

(iii) In developing countries like India where, for various social and economic reasons, preference is given to boys' education, any increase in fees would provide a disincentive to parents to send their daughters to colleges and this would retard the growth of girls' education.

(iv) In the current situation of student unrest, it would be unwise to give students further reason to protest and disturb academic life on university campuses.

To conclude: it is difficult to deny the validity of the arguments for and against raising the current level of the fees at the higher education stage. The crux of the problem, in the Indian situation, is that while the raising of fees is justified as a measure of mobilising the much needed additional resources,[6] such action should not restrict the flow of talented but economically disadvantaged students to institutions of higher education. Further, it should not appear as an anti-egalitarian measure and cause resentment on the part of the Indian people,[7] who are already suffering from a substantial rise in the cost of living. Considered in this context, an indiscriminate increase in tuition fees would not appear to be the answer.

A SUGGESTED PROGRAMME OF ACTION

When considering the totality of the Indian situation, a suggestion that merits serious consideration is the introduction of what may be called a 'differential' fee system, that is, higher fees (broadly on the cost of service principle), being charged to students who are not regarded as being suitable for higher education and the usual fees from those regarded as academically suitable—coupled with a large scholarship programme for this category of students. This would also necessitate special consideration for disadvantaged students.

There are a number of difficulties involved in implementing this type of reform. The main arguments against this proposal are that it is not practicable to introduce such a scheme on a large scale, and it is somewhat discriminatory. It is believed, however, that while this proposal may provoke opposition and may also result in some hardship to those intending to enter higher education, the long-term advantages of this proposal outweigh the disadvantages, and the suggested reform in the fee structure warrants serious consideration and implementation for a trial period.

Private Philanthropy

We have already discussed the problem inherent in, across the board, raising of fees although, on economic and educational grounds, the step is amply justified. An allied question is raising the contributions from private philanthropy which, for various reasons, have tended to decline in recent years. The qestion is important because in the present state of Indian economy, it is difficult to predict an era of abundance of resources for the educational institutions.

We had requested the principals of the colleges in the three states mentioned above whether they had attempted to raise private resources other than those provided by the society running the institution for maintenance/development of the institutions. Out of 84 institutions, which responded, 12 (13%) reported having made some effort to raise private resources. Further, except for Andhra Pradesh, the total quantum of resources generated through private effort was dismally small. Table 7.2 sums up the position:

TABLE 7.2 : **Mobilisation of private resources**

(Resources generated: 1976-77 to 1980-81)

State	Total number of colleges responding	Total number of colleges reporting resource mobilisation	Total (Rs. lakhs.)	Average per college per year
Andhra Pradesh	36	7	13.17	37,628
Gujarat	29	3	.35	2,330
Haryana	19	2	.63	6,300
Total	84	12	14.15	23,500

The main difficulties mentioned by the collegiate institutions in raising private resources are summarised below :

1. The donors put many conditions to be fulfilled by the institutions like giving their name to the buildings constructed with their contribution. These conditions cannot always be accepted.
2. Current economic difficulties resulting in rising costs of living particularly in rurals area militate against private resource mobilisation.
3. Donations are generally available for capital works rather than for running the institutions.
4. Maintenance of colleges is believed to be the responsibility of the government and not of the public.

Among the special measures to attract private contribution, the following may be mentioned.

(i) Approaching voluntary organisations:
(ii) Organising cultural programmes;
(iii) Special resources mobilisation campaigns and
(iv) Parent-teacher associations and alumni associations

It is recognised that in the present inflationary conditions, with the fast erosion in the individual incomes and the ever escalating costs of living, it is difficult to persuade the general public to donate to the educational institutions. It is, however, necessary that concerted efforts should be made to approach the community to donate for educational purposes. For this, the collegiate institutions will have to shed their policy of academic isolation and reach the community through personal contact programmes, students' participation in social service activities and so on. The main emphasis should be to make the society conscious of the educational requirements of the institutions, so that they could provide liberal assistance for the upkeep of the colleges. The programmes of contacting the community through institutional improvement conferences in Tamil Nadu and Maharashtra are an eloquent testimony to the success of this approach.

Before concluding the discussion about the community participation in the financing of institutions of higher education, we would like to condemn, in unequivocal terms, the practice of institutions in some states to charge huge amounts of money for admissions particularly to professional courses. This 'auctioning' of university places to the highest bidders is blatantly undemocratic, besides being highly unethical and immoral. This is also academically abnoxious in that it places a premium on the purchasing power of the students (or the parents) rather than on their intellectual endowments. We would rather prefer the university institutions to starve than to meet their needs through these nefarious means.

NOTES AND REFERENCES

1. Education Commission (1964-66), op. cit. p. 328.
2. For details, see D.M. Nanjundappa, *Working of University Finances*, Sterling Publishers, New Delhi, 1976, p. 348-60.
3. Ibid., p. 353.
4. The information presented in this paragraph is taken mainly from *The World Survey of Education* : IV (UNESCO, 1966).
5. On the contrary, there is a tendency on the part of a number of States to abolish all fees.
6. The suggestion for raising fees has been repeated time and again. The National Seminar on College and University Finances held in 1978 pleaded for establishing some relationship between what a student pays and what is spent on him. Recently, the National Policy Resolution issued by the Government of India stressed the need for charging fees in secondary and higher education stages from those sections of population, who are in a position to pay at rates, which bear reasonable relationship to the cost of providing education (National Policy Resolution, Government of India, 1979, p. 22).
7. In our study, while about 46 per cent of the respondents underlined the desirability of raising fees at the higher education stage, only 32 per cent were of the view that such an enhancement would be possible in conditions obtaining at present in India.

8

CONCLUSIONS AND POLICY IMPLICATION

WE HAVE attempted, in the preceding chapters, to bring to focus the major contours of the system of financing of higher education in India, with particular reference to the policies and procedures of grant-in-aid evolved by the federal and state governments. Our analysis has revealed certain distortions and inconsistencies in the behaviour of university finances. Before presenting an over-view of the major findings of this study, it appears pertinent to point out that the system of higher education has been subjected to a sort of ambivalent attitude on the part of the government and other funding bodies. This is partly because of the feeling in certain quarters that higher education is, by and large, an instrument of perpetuating social inequalities. It is considered as a vestige of the privileged—a prerogative of the upper middle elitist groups.

In sharp contrast to this, school education, particularly for children up to the age of 14 years, has been considered in conformity with egalitarianism, and equality of opportunity—the professed principles of Indian polity. It has been argued, and not always without substance, that the bulk of the beneficiaries of higher education are the urban upper-middle classes and hence the state should not extend financial support to these groups, who can, in any case, fend for themselves. Contriwise, elementary education caters to the large body of under-privileged children who have been denied even the modicum of educational facilitics for centuries. This bias against higher education persists notwithstanding the fact that university education plays a pivotal role in the production of technical and professional manpower, besides producing highly educated and cultured citizenry.

The dilemma facing the authorities concerned with the financing of educational programmes can be imagined by describing the two diametrically opposed scenarios that characterise Indian education in the present times. In the first scenario, one comes across a never-ending stream of young men and women knocking at the portals of university institutions. Quite a few of these aspirants for higher education have no better reason to be in universities and colleges than that they have no alternative to utilise their time. In the other scenario, one finds hesitation and reluctance writ large on the faces of a large body of parents to commit their children to the school system—formal or non-formal. Most of these parents belong to the socially and economically weaker sections of the society.

The system of financing of the educational programmes has, therefore, to steer clear of these apparently dichotomous situations. The self-expanding system of higher education has to be restrained—without compromising its potentiality to produce the scientific and professional manpower. The slow moving system of school education, particularly at the elementary stage, has to be accelerated by providing schooling facilities within a reasonable distance in habitations and through various schemes of incentives to pupils belonging to the poorer families.

To achieve the delicate balance between the conflicting claims of the two educational scenarios would require a rare combination of human ingenuity, administrative acumen and tact-attributes, which the bureaucrats concerned with the allocation of resources for education are not always endowed with. If, in the process, distortions in the financing of educational programmes occur, the reasons would not be far to seek.

In the context of the above remarks, it is proposed to summarise below the major conclusions of this study. In the latter part of this chapter, the policy implications and suggestions for revamping the system of government support for higher education will be given.

CONCLUSIONS

Aggregative expenditure

The ambivalence in the government attitude towards financing of higher education is reflected in the behaviour of aggregative expenditure on institutions of higher education. In spite of a substantial increase in the overall expenditure on education as well as higher education in the post-independence period, it is difficult to vouchsafe the adequacy or otherwise of the financial inputs in education and higher education. In fact, a study of the financial position of a cross-section of universities has revealed that financial inputs have not been adequate to meet the requirements of these institutions. The inadequacy of finances has been further accentuated by the spiralling inflation that has overtaken the economy during the past decade or so.

Inter-sectoral priorities

There have been substantial shifts in the inter-sectoral priorities under the successive five year plans. In the first plan, elementary education was given more than half of the allocable resources for educational development. University education was kept at a comparatively lower position. From the second plan to the fifth plan, university education received adequate priority as compared to other sectors like elementary and secondary education. In the sixth plan, however, the pendulum seems to have swung to the other extreme; higher education has been given almost the same position as in the second plan. It is, however, doubtful to forecast with a fair degree of accuracy whether the sectors like elementary and adult education will be able to maintain the priority accorded to them.

Contrary to the common belief, it has been revealed that higher education has not been receiving any preferential treatment in the allocation of resources. An analysis of the overall sectorwise budgetted outlays and actual expenditures has revealed that there are no diversion of resources from other sectors to higher education. In fact, if there are diversions, they are from programmes like scholarships and fellowships, cultural activities, games and sports and so on. Higher education sector is as much susceptible to diversions of resources as other sectors of education.

Within the university system, the central universities have appropriated the largest federal subventions, while the state universities have to be content with a much smaller share of the governments' munificence. There are some reasons for this invidious financial discrimination but they neither explain nor validate this phenomenon. The colleges of general education are also victims of indifference on the part of the federal as well as the state governments. Besides inadequate resources, there are certain other problems also thwarting the development of collegiate institutions. We shall have occasion to discuss them briefly in the latter part of this chapter.

State expenditures

The behaviour of sectoral expenditures under the state governments indicates an erratic and inconsistent configuration. No definite trend has been observed in the inter-state variations in the per capita expenditure on education as well as its break-up among different sectors of education. Further, while the coefficients of correlation between the states' net domestic product and the per capita expenditure on education as a whole have been significant, in the case of higher education, the degree of relationship has tended to decline substantially. This indicates that the expenditure on higher education has not kept pace with the changes in the net domestic product of the state governments over the years.

Sources of finance

The government has emerged, over the years, as the largest contributor to university and college finances. Private contributions, that is, tuition fees and private benefactions, have declined perceptibly.

Efficiency of higher educat ion

Due to inadequacy of resources and a number of socio-political factors, on some of whom the university ir stitutions have no control, the system of higher education has been working with much less than the optimum level of efficiency. The huge wastage and stagnation that occurs at this stage as also the ever-increasing unemployment among the university graduates and post-graduates, indicates, among other things, the loss of scarce financial resources that are made available to institutions of higher education.

Grant-in-aid from state governments

General conditions

The system of state grants which has been in existence from the time of the East India Company's Despatch of 1854 has undergone considerable changes. The state governments have laid down fairly comprehensive conditions of grant-in-aid. These conditions pertain to institutional expansion, appointment of managing committees, creation of reserve fund, construction of buildings, participation of staff in political activities, student discipline, religious neutrality and so on. Most of the state governments insist upon a period of probation for the colleges to be eligible for state assistance. This period may, in certain cases, extend to as long as nine years. Rules have been framed regulating student fees, qualifications of staff and enrolments etc.

An analysis of the conditions of grants laid down by the state governments reveals that main thrust of these conditions is on administrative and financial aspects, rather than on academic improvement of institutions. Quite a few of these conditions are not conducive to the academic development of the institutions. The conditions are half-heartedly enforced with the result that they fail to become effective instruments for the coordinated development of higher education.

The definitions of approved income and expenditure vary from state to state. In quite a few cases, some of the essential items, which have a bearing on the standards of educational facilities, do not find a place in the list of approved items.

Patterns and procedures

The patterns and procedures of assistance from the state governments to collegiate institutions vary substantially from state to state. In order to assess the effectiveness of the patterns of state grants for maintaining the institutions and improving the quality of education, the system was examined in terms of certain parameters like equity, specificity, adequacy, elasticity and efficiency etc. The detailed findings have been given in the relevant chapter. Here it may be stated that the patterns and procedures of grants introduced by some state governments have been lacking in terms of one or more of the important parameters indicated above. The following is the summary of the major findings :

(a) The system is inequitable in that certain types of institutions are given grants on a more liberal scale than others. The wide variations in the patterns of grants introduced by various states also bring out the inter-state discrimination perpetrated against collegiate institutions.

(b) The system of grant-in-aid lacks specificity. To cite a few examples :

  (i) quite a few states have not framed grant-in-aid rules and have left the decision of such an important matter to the state bureaucracy;

  (ii) in a number of states, the terms approved income and expenditure have not been defined.

  (iii) some of the schemes of assistance are subject to arbitrary monetary ceilings.

(c) The inadequacy of central and state grants is revealed by the fact that two out of every five institutions, whose budgets were studied had no means of adequately meeting their requirements. In order to keep their expenditure within the ceilings prescribed by the central and state authorities, the institutions were forced to keep the posts vacant and apply ad-hoc reductions on development programmes etc.

(d) The grant-in-aid system is also non-promotional in that it offers no special encouragement to the institutions to show better performance in academic or co-curricular activities. Further, it does not provide adequate incentive to mobilise resources for higher education. On the other hand, in certain states, it discourages resource mobilisation by the institutions. For example some states have laid down that no college will be given grant-in-aid, if it has a surplus in hand of a specified amount. Further most of the states do not allow the institutions to raise tuition fees.

(e) It was also reported that certain procedures of state grants interfere with the autonomy of the university institutions. This was with particular reference to appointing teaching staff, determining courses of study and selecting students for various university courses.

(f) In the operation of grant-in-aid system, a large number of administrative and procedural bottlenecks have also been reported. More than half of the institutions, which were approached, testified to the delay in the assessment, sanction and release of the state grants.

Federal grants

The grants from the federal government are available through a large number of organisations set up by the government. These organisations have introduced their own systems of grants for the development of institutions as also for promotion of research. Although the federal agencies like the University Grants Commission, the Indian Council of Agricultural Research etc. have delineated policy guidelines for the development of higher education, its implementation depends upon the cooperation of the state governments, who are primarily responsible for the development of education, including higher education. This limits the effectiveness of the policy framework specified by the central organisations.

The main agency of the federal governments for giving assistance to the universities and colleges is the University Grant Commission. An analysis of the UGC's grants reveals that the bulk of resources made available by the UGC are to build up the physical infrastructural facilities of the universities and colleges. While the need for improving the physical facilities in the universities and colleges cannot be over-emphasised, it is also necessary to bring about a balance in the development of physical and human resources in university institutions. In that context, equal emphasis should be given to the quality of teaching personnel, incentives to meritorious students and so on.

The important problems emerging from the operation of the UGC grants are as follows:

(i) the UGC grants are *responsive* rather than promotional in that the Commission, by the large, reacts to the proposals submitted by the university institutions, rather than taking initiative in assessing the requirements of the universities and colleges on its own and providing assistance on the basis of that assessment. Even in the establishment of university institutions, the Commission's role is somewhat passive rather than active. This is because of the constitutional limitations on the role of the UGC under which the Commission is expected to give advice, *if such advice is asked for*, on the establishment of a new university. The position has not improved materially even by the amendment of the Act, under which the UGC can refuse grants, if its advice is not heeded.

(ii) the UGC has introduced a number of schemes, which could legitimately be left over to the state governments.

(iii) the financial assistance given by the UGC is inequitous in that it is more munificent to the universities, particularly to the central universities than to the colleges which are responsible for 83 per cent of the student enrolment. The grants also show wide state-wise variations in terms of per student average annual inputs.

(iv) most of the UGC's grants involve matching contribution from the state governments and/or institutions. Quite a few schemes fail to get implemented because of the inability or unwillingness of the states to provide their share.

Support for research

Support for research and development comes from a variety of federal agencies. Financial assistance is available for research projects, fellowships, scholarships and publications, etc. In a number of cases, the functions of the federal agencies are overlapping in character and there is no in-built mechanism of coordination and collaboration between the various agencies operating the schemes of grants for research. Here also, the funding agencies have adopted a passive role in that, by and large, they react to proposals rather than initiate them. The distribution of grants also lacks uniformity. Bulk of the available funds are appropriated by a few institutions and academics. The research projects take a very long time to be implemented because of, among other reasons, concentration of the bulk of projects at fewer places. The procedure for evaluation of programmes of assistance for research is somewhat cumbersome and dilatory.

POLICY IMPLICATIONS

We propose to discuss the policy implications of the role of the federal and the state governments in the financing of higher education on the basis of the following postulates:

(i) The government has a vital stake in the system of higher education for, among other things, its potentiality to produce high level technical and professional manpower.

(ii) Through historical and other reasons, private enterprise has entered the field of higher education in a big way. It has, however, been unable to provide adequate financial assistance of a recurrent nature. Hence quite a few of the privately managed institutions are running at less than the optimum level of efficiency.

(iii) In view of the significance of higher education for accelerating the process of socio-economic development, the government has to ensure adequate provision of financial assistance for the maintenance and development of these institutions. Further, the federal government has the constitutional responsibility of maintaining academic standards of institutions of higher education and research. This would necessitate the evolution of a well considered policy of financing of higher education consistent with the governments' responsibility for the development of other sectors of education, particularly elementary education.

The essential features of a policy framework for financing of higher education would be as follows:

1. Planning university development;
2. Streamlining financial procedures; and
3. Augmenting internal resources.

Planning university development

An integrated plan of university development would necessitate action on two counts:

(i) Regulating university expansion and
(ii) Institutional planning.

Regulating expansion

Much has been said about the need for controlling the unplanned expansion of student enrolment and restricting the proliferation of non-viable institutions. It is, however, difficult to place a moratorium on the expansion of higher education facilities. The problem is extremely complicated and hyper-sensitive in the Indian situation. Through a policy of expansion of elemantary education, educational facilities are becoming increasingly available to those sections of population, which never had any tradition of education in their families for centuries. Restriction of university enrolment would adversely affect these most vulnerable sections of the society, who are increasingly realising the need for education as a means of their socio-economic upliftment. We shall have, therefore, to tread cautiously. We suggest the following steps for achieving the desired objectives.

The aspirants for university education could be broadly classified into professional and non-professional students. We shall have to consider the enrolment policies about these two groups separately.

Professional courses

So far as professional courses are concerned, there can be no two opinions about the need for regulating the flow of students keeping in view the assessed manpower needs. For this purpose, various specialised bodies like the Indian Council of Agricultural Research, Planning Commission, All-India Council for Technical Education and the Institute of Applied Man-power Research have been making forecasts of the requirements of technical manpower in specialised disciplines from time to time. The attempts are, however, sporadic and of an *ad hoc* character. Further, there is no in-built mechanism of revising these forecasts, keeping in view the changes in the economy from time to time.

It is recognised that in a vast country like India with the constituent units having widely divergent rates of economic growth, provision of educational facilities and other social variates, it is difficult to impose a strait-jacket approach to monpower planning. The problem is also complicated because of the restrictive recruitment policies caused by the insistence on the knowledge of local languages or domiciliary restrictions, which restrict the mobility of technical personnel from one state to the other. There is, therefore, need for state-wise manpower forecasting for higher technical personnel and region-wise projections for lower level technicians. The need for evolving manpower strategies particularly for the highly trained scientific and technical manpower at the national level and tailoring the educational policies to achieve that end cannot, however, be undervalued.

Non-professional courses

In the case of admission to non-professional courses, a state of near chaos prevails. Here no holds are barred either in the admission of students or in the setting up of institutions. We have already discussed the extremely hyper-sensitive nature of this problem. A policy of restrictive admissions, across the board, is therefore out of question.

And yet from the point of view of educational finance, the problem cannot be brushed aside. The huge loss in human and physical resources must be avoided.

To achieve this objective, a somewhat different strategy should be put into operation for admission to non-professional courses. While the regular institutional facilities should be made available to the students, who show some merit, the vast bulk of the students, who are below standard, should be diverted to non-formal courses: correspondence courses, sandwich courses, evening colleges, and so on. They may also be allowed to take university examinations as external candidates. This would, however, necessitate making the system of non-formal education much more efficient than it is at present in India.

Institutional planning

Before discussing the scope of institutional planning, we would like to say a few words about the mechanism of planning of higher education.

Mechanism of planning

Planning of higher education, to be effective, has to be a joint enterprise of the federal and the state governments, universities and colleges. In this connection we do not agree to the suggestion made by the Review Committee on the University Grants Commission that the UGC should be made responsible for higher education planning of the country within the overall policy directions of the Ministry of Education. In the first instance, the UGC, constituted as it is, has a truncated responsibility in higher education. Its writ does not run beyond non-professional higher education. Further it has not developed any organic linkages with the other organisations like the Indian Council of Agricultural Research, All-India Council for Technical Education, Medical Council of India, and so on. Even with the Planning Commission, the UGC had over the years not been having "adequate continuing contact and dialogues. . . .!" In the absence of such a contact, it has not developed any intimate knowledge of the problems of professional institutions and the manpower needs of those disciplines. The UGC has also not developed any expertise for planning of higher education for which it is constitutionally responsible. We are inclined to agree to the apprehension of the Review Committee that "the UGC was drawing its programmes more or less in isolation and in an ad hoc manner."[2]

In view of all this, it would be difficult for the UGC or any central organisation to address itself effectively to the task of preparing a national plan of the development of higher education. There is, therefore, need for all the concerned organisations to pool their resources in the drawing up of a plan of development of higher education. The drawing up of an overall plan of university development will necessitate working out the model plans for individual university institutions. We shall briefly discuss below the mechanism of institutional planning.

Universities

The planning at the university level has to be all pervasive covering financial, administrative and academic aspects. It has been experienced that the universities generally wait for a suggestion from the UGC or the government to set their planning machinery into motion. In the process, quite a bit of valuable time is lost and, because of paucity of time, the plan that emerges is more in the nature of a string of disjointed programmes rather than a well thought out coordinated plan.

A good plan will necessitate a very sound data base covering progress achieved in various departments, the bottlenecks discovered and the capacity of the various departments for further growth. The data needs should also include the progress achieved by the colleges affiliated to the university, the difficulties faced by them in implementing developmental programmes and the likely rise in enrolment extrapolated on a fairly long-term basis. The university should also undertake studies of unit costs in respect of various constituents of the educational expenditure so that realistic cost estimates could be worked out. In view of the uncertainties of the financial situation, each university should also keep in readiness a contingent plan so that in case the plan as originally envisaged cannot be implemented, they have not to resort to a make-shift plan, which may not be conducive to the development of higher education.

Colleges

An important constituent of planning relates to a close and continuous overview of the opening of collegiate institutions. At present the universities are, by and large, passive spectators in the process of the proliferation of colleges particularly under private auspices. Here the initiative generally lies with an individual or an organisation, which realises the need for the setting up of a collegiate institution. Many a time, the decision to start a college is taken on extra-academic considerations. The colleges are set up and then they apply for affiliation to the universities. At that stage—which is rather late—the university puts its evaluative machinery into action. More often than not, the conditions of affiliation, which, at least theoretically, are quite inconvenient (like the putting up of adequate buildings, creation of reserve fund etc.) are circumvented through the grant of temporary affiliation. This temporary affiliation has the potentiality of continuing indefinitely. In the process, very often, non-viable institutions come into being and continue to exist.

To bring about planned expansion and development of collegiate institutions, we would commend the scheme suggested by the Committee on College Finances (1977)[3] appointed by the Gujarat State. The main constituents of the scheme are:

(i) there should be a single authority for the state as a whole, which should decide whether a new college should or should not be located at a given place. No university in the state should entertain application for the affiliation of a new college unless the need for such college has been certified by this authority, which will lay down criteria for the establishment of new colleges.

(ii) no new college should be permitted except in areas where the existing facilities for higher education are inadequate and where a clear case exists for the establishment of new institution.

(iii) the rules for grant of affiliation should lay down that the management of a college should raise a sum of not less than Rs. 5 lakhs for buildings and equipment and another sum of not less than Rs. 5 lakhs as an endowment fund before its application for affiliation is granted.

(iv) it should be the policy of the government as well as of the management to make every college viable.

Streamlining financial procedures

Assuming that the present unplanned state of affairs in the expansion of higher education will give place to a system of planned development, it is the responsibility of the federal and state governments to ensure a sound financial base for the universities and colleges.

Role of federal and state governments

The first step in this direction is the delineation of the respective responsibilities of the federal and the state governments. In spite of the somewhat ambiguous character of the federal responsibility in the field of higher education in that "coordination and determination of standards of higher education and research" is capable of multiple interpretations, it is necessary that the overlap in the financial policies of the federal and state governments should be avoided. What appears logical is that the federal government should concern itself mainly with post-graduate education and research and provide full financial assistance for its development. Under-graduate education should appropriately be left to the state governments. The federal agencies may, subject to availability of funds, provide assistance for certain specific schemes of development of undergraduate education.

Patterns and procedures of grants

There is also need for a national consensus about the procedures of financing institutions of higher education. The consensus should involve determination of the items that form a part of the admissible expenditure. As has been observed in the preceding analysis, there are wide divergences in the definition of such items.

Incentive grants

The question of the pattern of grants is also an important consideration. We have seen that the prevalent pattern in most of the states is the 'deficit' system of assistance. While it is a reasonably good measure of assessing the financial needs of institutions, it has to be supplemented by a system of incentive grants, which will mean giving additional assistance for good performance. We have made suggestion about evaluating performance. Here also the question may be determined on an all-India level.

Grants for research

Grants for research are available from a number of organisations. While it is beyond the scope of this discussion to question the desirability of having so many organisations, some of which are having overlapping functions, it is necessary that these organisations should streamline their procedures and policies through a continuing dialogue among themselves. At present, most of these organisations are working in a state of splendid academic isolation, jealously guarding themselves against any instrusions—imaginary or real—in their autonomy. As we have already argued, autonomy is a means rather than an end. It should be an instrument of better financial and academic management rather than a factor inhibiting the proper growth of higher education.

It is also necessary that a closer look be given to the researches undertaken in the university and non-university institutions. It is difficult to make any general observations about the quantity and quality of research in various disciplines in the Indian universities. Some of our researches can stand any international comparisons. On the other hand, there is also some truth in the statement that quite a sizeable research at the university stage is traditional and stereo-typed. For example, in the field of education, it has been found that researches in the newly emerging areas of educational planning, finance and administration are few and far between.

We had examined[4] the researches in education conducted by the Indian universities during the years 1981 and 1982. It was revealed that out of 148 researches completed for the award of Ph.D. degree only 7 related to the area of economics of education. Out of this, only two were concerning educational finance. It appears that due to various reasons, including lack of appropriate expertise, the universities prefer to tread on familiar ground rather than opening up new vistas of research.

The point that needs to be made is that research in the university system should be on the basis of a well thought out policy of promoting research, which should be relevant to the needs of the society. The newly emerging areas in different disciplines should be given due emphasis. Stress should be laid on inter-disciplinary research rather than the various departments working in water-tight compartments.

There should also be a system of inter-varsity communication about the researches under way and those completed. There should also be some arrangement for widely circulating the findings of the researches completed at the various university centres.

STATE LEVEL GRANT GIVING BODIES

The streamlining of the procedures of grants at the state level will not be possible unless academic organisations on the pattern of the federal bodies are created at the state level. Whether it should be designated as state university grants committees or committees for higher education is immaterial. What matters is the emergence of an academic organisation to be interposed between the state bureaucracy and the university institutions. While making this suggestion, we are not unmindful of the somewhat discouraging experience of some of the state governments that had ventured to set up such bodies. This should not, however, under-value the need for such bodies at the state level.

It may be mentioned that the University Education Commission (1948-49) under the Chairmanship of late Dr. S. Radhakrishnan, which had recommended the establishment of the central UGC, had also suggested the setting up of the state grants allocation committees on the lines of the central UGC. The suggestion made by this Commission is valid even today and should be implemented without any further loss of time; the reservations of the Education Commission (1964-66) notwithstanding.

Augmenting resources

We have to reckon with the fact that, for a long time to come, the resources available for education as well as higher education would be scarce and hence there would be need for augmenting resources from non-government sources. We have discussed the problems involved in the raising of tuition fees. We firmly believe that the fee-structure should have some relationship with the costs of university education. Higher education is not a prerogative of every body and those, who can pay, should be made to pay sizeable proportion of recurring costs. This should, however, be supplemented by a programme of scholarships and freeships for meritorious, but financially weaker sections of society.

There is also need for harnessing private resources for the maintenance and development of collegiate institutions. In this connection two proposals are worth considering. Firstly, there should be no ceiling on tax remission for financial contribution to educational institutions. Secondly, legislative measures may be adopted requiring private/public enterprises, particularly users of technically trained personnel to contribute a fixed portion of their profits for educational purposes.

No proposal for harnessing public support for collegiate institutions is likely to be effective unless the university institutions establish living contact with the community around them. They should become centres of community life and share their problems with the people around them. It is only through becoming relevant to the community that the colleges and universities can expect large public contributions for their maintenance and development. The school improvement conferences organised by the Tamil Nadu Government and also a few other states speak volumes about the rich dividents that institutional contacts with the community bring in their wake.

To conclude

It may be stated that the conclusions and policy implications mentioned in this chapter are, by and large, based largely on a macro-analysis of the system of financing of higher education. They are meant to present a gestalt view of the working of financing of the university institutions, the varying dimensions of financial inputs over the years, the divergent policies and patterns of federal and state grants and so on. The suggestions made in this study are expected to help the federal and the state agencies to streamline their funding policies.

In order to percieve the financial system in its variegated configurations, it would be necessary to undertake in-depth studies of the financial policies of the federal and state governments. It may also be useful to study the impact of these policies and procedures on the development of institutions of higher education. Studies may also be undertaken of finances of individual universities and colleges of various types in order to identify the problems facing these institutions.

It may, however, be emphasised that the financial system pertaining to the university institutions can admit of no single remedy; it will have to be a judicious mixture of a series of measures for streamlining the financial system of university institutions. For achieving this, a number of experimental studies will have to be undertaken.

NOTES AND REFERENCES

1. Review Committee on UGC, op. cit., p. 74.
2. Ibid., p. 74.
3. Committee on College Finances, Government of Gujarat, Ahmedabad, 1977, p. 48.
4. See the authors' paper : Researches in Educational Finance; Problems and Perspectives—1982 (Mimeo).

APPENDICES

APPENDIX I(i)

STATE-WISE PER CAPITA N.D.P. AND ITS RELATIONSHIP WITH EXPENDITURE ON EDUCATION

(*Expenditure in Rs.*)

State	Per capita NDP	Rank	Per capita expenditure on education	Rank	Per capita expenditure on elementary education	Rank	Per capita expenditure on secondary education	Rank	Per capita expenditure on higher education	Rank
1	2	3	4	5	6	7	8	9	10	11
Andhra Pradesh	275	9	7.10	9	2.90	9	1.49	9	1.09	8
Assam	315	6	7.60	7	3.49	7	1.71	7	0.97	12
Bihar	215	15	4.90	14	1.73	13	0.76	14	0.60	14
Gujarat	362	3	9.20	6	5.17	3	1.61	8	1.55	4
Jammu & Kashmir	269	10	5.70	12	0.91	15	1.81	6	0.99	11
Kerala	259	12	11.50	2	5.58	1	2.54	2	1.23	5
Karnataka	286	7	7.50	8	3.90	6	1.01	12	1.10	7
Madhya Pradesh	260	11	6.20	11	3.01	8	0.94	13	1.05	10
Maharashtra	409	1	12.40	1	5.42	2	2.38	3	1.60	3
Orissa	216	14	4.30	15	1.51	14	0.50	15	0.43	15
Punjab	347	4	9.30	5	4.92	4	4.05	1	3.08	1
Rajasthan	284	8	6.30	10	2.73	11	1.22	11	0.91	13
Tamil Nadu	334	5	9.40	4	4.06	5	1.84	5	1.21	6

1	2	3	4	5	6	7	8	9	10	11
Uttar Pradesh	252	13	5.40	13	2.87	10	1.28	10	1.08	9
West Bengal	290	2	9.80	3	2.02	12	2.16	4	1.89	2
Mean	298.2		7.77		3.35		1.69		1.25	
Standard deviation	37.31		2.34		1.43		0.85		0.60	
Coefficient of variation	19.22		30.07		42.69		50.10		48.00	
Rank correlation (with per capita NDP)			0.78		0.50		0.63		0.74	

APPENDIX I(ii)

STATE-WISE PER CAPITA N.D.P. AND ITS RELATIONSHIP WITH EXPENDITURE ON EDUCATION: (1965-66)

(*Expenditure in Rs.*)

State	Per capita NDP	Rank	Per capita expenditure on education	Rank	Per capita expenditure on elementary education	Rank	Per capita expenditure on secondary education	Rank	Per capita expenditure on higher education	Rank
1	2	3	4	5	6	7	8	9	10	11
Andhra Pradesh	383	7	10.7	11	3.87	13	2.63	9	2.41	9
Assam	399	6	12.4	9	6.62	5	2.67	8	1.77	13
Bihar	332	12	6.3	15	2.36	15	1.04	15	1.45	14
Gujarat	498	4	14.7	6	7.79	1	3.42	6	3.32	3
Jammu & Kashmir	317	14	14.3	7	4.11	11	3.20	7	3.18	4
Kerala	380	9	19.5	1	7.57	2	4.48	1	2.90	5
Madhya Pradesh	305	15	11.4	10	4.49	9	1.80	13	2.26	11
Tamil Nadu	403	5	16.5	3	7.32	3	3.62	5	2.46	8
Maharashtra	534	1	17.5	2	7.18	4	3.95	3	2.87	6
Karnataka	386	8	13.0	8	6.21	6	1.97	12	2.69	7
Orissa	329	13	8.5	14	3.32	14	1.16	14	1.35	15
Punjab	532	2	16.0	4	4.47	10	3.86	4	4.07	1
Rajasthan	373	10	10.1	12	5.18	8	2.15	10	2.32	10

1	2	3	4	5	6	7	8	9	10	11
Uttar Pradesh	373	10	8.8	13	5.29	7	2.04	11	1.98	12
West Bengal	532	2	15.1	5	4.06	12	4.06	2	3.36	2
Mean	398.7		12.99		5.35		2.80		2.56	
Standard deviation	77.65		3.17		1.63		1.05		0.73	
Coefficient of variation	19.48		24.40		30.50		37.50		28.52	
Rank correlation (with per capita N.D.P.)			0.63		0.39		0.21		0.58	

APPENDIX I(iii)

STATE-WISE PER CAPITA N.D.P. AND ITS RELATIONSHIP WITH EXPENDITURE ON EDUCATION: (1970-71)

(*Expenditure in Rs.*)

State	Per capita NDP	Rank	Per capita expenditure on education	Rank	Per capita expenditure on elementary education	Rank	Per capita expenditure on secondary education	Rank	Per capita expenditure on higher education	Rank
1	2	3	4	5	6	7	8	9	10	11
Andhra Pradesh	565	9	15.55	12	5.77	8	4.21	10	2.40	8
Assam	528	11	18.93	7	6.55	6	5.15	9	2.42	7
Bihar	426	16	10.03	15	5.54	11	1.09	16	1.18	15
Gujarat	843	3	17.70	10	8.61	4	4.15	11	1.96	13
Haryana	845	2	19.66	5	4.42	13	9.82	2	2.73	4
Jammu & Kashmir	524	12	19.12	6	3.80	16	7.66	3	3.94	1
Kerala	586	8	31.09	1	16.21	1	5.84	6	3.09	3
Madhya Pradesh	490	15	15.41	13	5.19	12	3.88	12	1.83	14
Maharashtra	799	4	20.73	3	9.21	2	6 48	4	2.06	11
Karnataka	540	10	18.91	8	8.64	3	3.78	13	2.34	9
Orissa	493	14	13.60	14	14.35	14	3.50	14	2.15	10
Punjab	986	1	23.12	2	5.66	9	10.79	1	3.68	2
Rajasthan	623	6	16.75	11	5.80	7	6.13	5	2.51	6

1	2	3	4	5	6	7	8	9	10	11
Tamil Nadu	618	7	19.73	4	7.90	5	5.23	8	1.98	12
Uttar Pradesh	504	13	9.33	16	4.07	15	2.41	15	1.41	16
West Bengal	742	5	18.46	9	5.56	10	5.35	7	2.63	5
Mean	633.3		18.10		7.33		5.33		2.38	
Standard deviation	155.93		4.91		3.41		2.45		0.74	
Coefficient of variation	24.62		27.26		46.52		45.97		31.09	
Rank correlation (with per capita NDP)	—		0.65		0.42		0.73		0.46	

APPENDIX I(iv)

STATE-WISE PER-CAPITA N.D.P. AND ITS RELATIONSHIP WITH EXPENDITURE ON EDUCATION: (1975-76)

(*Expenditure in Rs,*)

State	Per capita NDP	Rank	Per capita expenditure on education	Rank	Per capita expenditure on elementary education	Rank	Per capita expenditure on secondary education	Rank	Per capita expenditure on university education	Rank
1	2	3	4	5	6	7	8	9	10	11
Andhra Pradesh	919	8	29.71	10	9.87	15	7.47	12	4.68	6
Assam	850	11	29.44	11	13.10	10	8.25	11	3.29	11
Bihar	868	17	18.23	17	10.00	14	3.08	17	3.16	12
Gujarat	1,038	6	29.95	9	14.38	7	8.68	9	3.15	13
Haryana	1,260	3	35.93	6	12.63	11	12.15	5	3.58	8
Himachal Pradesh	1050	4	62.95	1	27.35	2	21.86	1	6.16	2
Jammu & Kashmir	883	9	41.35	4	13.71	9	17.96	2	5.47	4
Karnataka	785	14	34.31	7	15.91	4	6.64	15	5.48	3
Kerala	950	7	59.22	2	31.05	1	13.63	4	8.15	1
Madhya Pradesh	793	13	25.48	15	10.40	13	7.45	13	2.70	16
Maharashtra	1,330	2	40.96	5	17.42	3	12.15	5	3.13	14
Orissa	785	14	26.57	13	9.51	17	8.49	10	3.37	9
Punjab	1,580	1	46.38	3	15.26	6	17.55	3	4.87	5
Rajasthan	850	11	29.16	12	15.46	5	7.17	14	3.30	10

1	2	3	4	5	6	7	8	9	10	11
Tamil Nadu	851	10	32.15	8	14.29	8	8.85	8	3.12	15
Uttar Pradesh	781	16	23.86	16	11.86	12	9.43	16	2.36	17
West Bengal	1,046	5	26.21	14	9.70	16	9.35	7	4.26	7
Mean	977.6		34.84		14.82		10.36		4.13	
Standard deviation	17.07		11.73		5.78		4.80		1.42	
Coefficient of variation	22.20		33.67		29.00		46.33		34.38	
Rank correlation (with per capita N.D.P.)	—		0.71		0.42		0.82		0.37	

APPENDIX I(v)

STATE-WISE PER CAPITA N.D.P. AND ITS RELATIONSHIP WITH EXPENDITURE ON EDUCATION: (1980-81)

(Expenditure in Rs.)

State	Per capita NDP	Rank	Per capita expenditure on education	Rank	Per capita expenditure on elementary education	Rank	Per capita expenditure on secondary education	Rank	Per capita expenditure on higher education	Rank
1	2	3	4	5	6	7	8	9	10	11
Andhra Pradesh	1,313	9	48.71	10	17.81	12	12.11	11	8.19	5
Bihar	870	15	36.95	13	20.91	9	5.74	15	4.70	11
Gujarat	1,896	4	53.59	7	27.01	4	15.41	7	4.24	13
Haryana	2,335	2	57.98	5	20.36	10	21.55	4	7.90	7
Himachal Pradesh	1,458	7	101.52	1	46.70	1	33.60	1	8.28	4
Karnataka	1,352	8	50.00	9	24.20	6	9.65	13	7.73	9
Kerala	1,312	10	92.83	2	46.66	2	22.73	3	8.91	1
Madhya Pradesh	1,177	13	34.59	14	14.91	14	10.69	12	3.57	14
Maharashtra	2,277	3	59.65	4	28.57	3	20.17	5	8.42	3
Orissa	1,147	14	43.32	12	16.49	13	14.99	8	5.12	10
Punjab	2,768	1	66.25	3	25.84	5	33.45	2	8.15	6
Rajasthan	1,203	12	44.81	11	22.61	7	13.12	10	4.50	12

1	2	3	4	5	6	7	8	9	10	11
Tamil Nadu	1,269	11	50.82	8	22.56	8	13.26	9	8.75	2
Uttar Pradesh	1,772	5	31.00	15	14.82	15	9.09	14	3.03	15
West Bengal	1,545	6	53.14	6	18.93	11	17.00	6	7.76	8
Mean	1579.60		55.01		24.56		16.84		6.62	
Standard deviation	510.42		18.97		9.56		7.97		2.05	
coefficient of Variation	32.31		34.48		38.93		47.33		30.97	
Rank correlation (with per capita N.D.P.)	.56		0.56		0.30		0.54		0.19	

APPENDIX II

SOURCE OF FINANCE OF VARIOUS TYPES OF COLLEGIATE INSTITUTIONS IN SOME STATES

(*Figures in percentages*)

Recurring income	Private General Education Colleges								
	Central Govt.	UGC	State Govt.	University	Local board	Fees	Endow-ments	Other sources	Total
Andhra Pradesh									
1976-77	0.09	0.62	71.67	—	—	24.46	0.08	3.08	100.00
1980-81	0.55	3.06	66.34	0.01	0.01	26.33	—	3.70	100.00
Gujarat									
1976-77	—	0.05	23.12	—	0.11	70.62	0.03	6.07	100.00
1980-81	—	0.01	57.13	—	1.14	36.44	0.02	5.26	100.00
Haryana									
1976-77	—	0.37	24.80	—	1.92	57.40	6.99	8.52	100.00
1980-81	—	4.91	40.60	0.04	0.88	41.17	6.25	6.15	100.00

APPENDIX III

PATTERNS OF STATE GRANT-IN-AID FOR INSTITUTIONS OF HIGHER EDUCATION

State	Maintenance grants	Building/hostel grants	Equipment grants	Other grants	Remarks
1	2	3	4	5	6
Andhra Pradesh	*Teaching Grants*: 100% Expenditure on salaries of teaching and non-teaching staff minus fees at standard rates to be limited to actual deficit, subject to the condition that existing rates of fees (1963-64) shall not be reduced.	*Buildings*: *First Grade Colleges* 50% subject to a maximum of Rs. 75,000 *Second Grade Colleges* 50% subject to a maximum of Rs. 50,000 *Hostel*: 50% of the total expenditure after deducting the rent received from the inmates.	*Furniture, Books, Appliances, etc.* 50% subject to a maximum of Rs. 10,000	1. *Ad hoc Grants* to unaided colleges preferably located in backward areas or women's and rural colleges for expenditure other than salary of staff. 2. *Fee Compensation Grants* 100% of loss incurred on fee concession to Scheduled Castes/ Backward Classes and tribal students.	From the year 1981-82, all the colleges having 80% aided posts are brought under the new scheme of payment of salaries through the banks.

State	Maintenance grants	Building/hostel grants	Equipment grants	Other grants	Remarks
1	2	3	4	5	6
Assam	The Government meets 100% of the deficit calculated in the manner indicated hereunder minus 30% of the monthly fee income which will be set apart for fee remission, building repairs, furniture, libraries to be determined by multiplying the number of students by the rates of fees and then deducting 30% of the total fee income; or in other words, 70% of the amount due on account of fees: $\frac{\text{(Rate of fee} \times \text{No. of students} \times 70}{100}$				A college to be eligible for grant-in-aid should have the following minimum enrolments: *Degree Colleges*: (a) Arts 300 (b) Science 120 (Relaxable in the case of Girls' Colleges).

1	2	3	4	5	6
Bihar	Grant-in-aid to the colleges is given on the recommendations of the university on the basis of the budget estimates of the colleges and the quality of work done. No fixed rules for grants to private colleges. The cases for financial assistance are decided on individual merit.				
Gujarat	*Pay Packet Grant* Grant-in-aid on pay packet should be equal to the difference between the total pay packet of approved staff in approved pay-scales—teaching and non—teaching staff—and the amount of tuition fees deemed to be collected. The pay packet includes pay,	Grant for repairs of building subject to the limits prescribed by the government.	*Laboratory Grants*: 50% of the excess expenditure over income from laboratory fees. Laboratory fees: Rs. 50 per student per term.	*Performance Grants*: Every College should introduce a system of institutional planning on the basis of over all comprehensive assessment of their progress in academic and extra-curricular	1. The maximum enrolment in a college should be 1,650. In a three-faculty college, it could be raised to 2,000 with the approval of the university. In the case of colleges located in cities with a population of one lakh and

State	Maintenance grants	Building/hostel grants	Equipment grants	Other grants	Remarks
1	2	3	4	5	6
	dearness and other allowances and contribution of the institution to provident fund of the teaching and non-teaching staff. The work load of lecturers will be calculated at 16 periods per week. The ratio of teaching and non-teaching staff is also fixed. *Development Grants*: (i) 25% grant on schemes sponsored by the U.G.C. (ii) 50% grant for enabling the colleges to develop on a planned basis so that it acquires a sort of individuality by way of specialisa-			activities. First three colleges should be given performance awards of Rs. 1,00,000 Rs. 75,000 and Rs. 50,000 respectively. The performance should be evaluated by proposed Gujarat Affiliated Colleges Board. Special Grants for providing special tuition and guidance to Scheduled Tribe students.	above, the minimum enrolment should be 3,00, 500 and 700 in single, double and triple faculty colleges respectively. The corresponding figures for colleges in cities with a population of less than one lakh or rural areas should be 200, 350 and 500 respectively. 2. In colleges, with less than the prescribed enrolment even after a three year period (ending 1980), the fee income will be calculated on the basis of prescribed

1	2	3	4	5	6
	tion in a particular major field. (iii) Grants at the rate to be prescribed by the State Government for faculty development and student services etc.				minimum enrolment. 3. A uniform tuition fee of Rs. 200 per student per term should be charged in undergraduate classes and Rs. 250 in colleges of education. 4. If a college levies higher fees, the extra amount should be utilised for developmental purposes.
Haryana	No fixed percentage laid down. All affiliated colleges will be eligible for grants to be awarded on the basis of deficit in expenditure on staff and contingencies and income from fees during the	No capital expenditure shall be considered in the calculations for grants. However, grants are given to private colleges for development		Grants at the rate of Rs. 3,000 each to women's colleges and those in rural areas.	(a) Subject to availability of funds for new colleges, grant-in-aid may be given up to Rs. 1 lakh for women's colleges and Rs. 50,000 for men's colleges

State	Maintenance grants	Building/hostel grants	Equipment grants	Other grants	Remarks
1	2	3	4	5	6
	previous year (subject to the availability of funds). No grant will be given to a college having no deficit. The grant-in-aid to the B.Ed. colleges is 95% of the net deficit.	purposes, which also cover hostel buildings.			and co-educational institutions. (b) Grants on account of revision of pay scale up to 100% of the additional expenditure. (c) Grants for DA in respect of persons whose pay has been adversely effected due to revision of pay scales.
Himachal Pradesh	No fixed percentage. Grant-in-aid to private affiliated colleges is given on the basis of deficit calculated on actual expenditurc on salary and contingencies and income from			Grants on account of revision of pay-scales up to 100% of the additional expenditure.	

1	2	3	4	5	6
	fees, donations etc. of the previous year, subject to budget provisions. No grant, if no deficit.				
Jammu & Kashmir	*Maintenance Grants*: The total grant on maintenance of an institution including all aid from public revenues towards expenditure on tuition shall not exceed the amount (to be fixed later) of excess of the expenditure on tuition over the income from tuition fees and endowments. *Staff Grants*: will be admissible to institutions that engage trained hands and work satisfactorily.	To be specified by the State Government.			Block grants will be given for quantitative and qualitative aspects of educational programmes conducted by the institutions based on general tuitional condition, percentage of results in the University/Board examination, use of library books by students, curricular activities by students, social welfare service and attendance of students. For this purpose, institutions

State	Maintenance grants	Building/hostel grants	Equipment grants	Other grants	Remarks
1	2	3	4	5	6
					are classified as first, second and third grade and the rate of block grants will be fixed, separately for each class of institutions.
Karnataka	The Director shall pay to the management 'salary grant' equal to the salaries and allowances of such employees as may be approved by the Director from time to time, at the same rates as prescribed for similar appointments under the government. The Director shall also prescribe minimum qualifications and				1. Management may collect tuition and laboratory fees at rates not exceeding twice the standard rates prescribed by the Government. This will be deposited in a joint account to be operated by the Director of Education and the college principal. 2. The management may also collect

1	2	3	4	5	6
	minimum hours of instruction for full time and part time employees.				fees for specific purposes like library, college examination, medical examination, sports etc. The amount in excess of standard rates and all specific and miscellaneous fees shall be put in a separate account called college account. Out of this, the management will meet 3% of the basic salary of the staff as triple benefit scheme and also the current maintenance expenditure, contingencies, consumable items etc.

State	Maintenance grants	Building/hostel grants	Equipment grants	Other grants	Remarks
1	2	3	4	5	6
					3. No employee will engage himself in any demonstration prejudical to the sovereignty and integrity of India, the security of the State, decency or morality etc. He will also not associate himself with any political party or organisation. He will also not contest any election or become a member of any House of Legislature or Parliament or local authority. 4. The management shall not take part in any political agitation directed

1	2	3	4	5	6
					against the authority of the State Government or foster opinion tending to excite feelings of disloyalty or disaffection among the students.
Kerala	There is no grant-in-aid system existing consequent upon the introduction of direct payment of pay and allowances to the teaching and non-teaching staff of the institution through the principal of the institution with effect from 1-9-1972 in arts and science colleges and with effect from 1-6-1973 in training colleges. Thus teaching grant has been replac-	Grant for the repair and maintenance of buildings to be calculated on a per capita basis subject to a ceiling to be fixed by the government separately for arts sections, science sections etc.	Grants for libraries and laboratories to be based on norms worked out in consultation with the Universities.	The Government shall pay contingency grant calculated on a per capita basis subject to a ceiling to be decided by the government.	1. The educational agency (management) shall collect tuition fees as prescribed and fines imposed on the students and remit all such amounts to the credit of the government. 2. The educational agency shall collect special fees at rates prescribed by the university and

State	Maintenance grants	Building/hostel grants	Equipment grants	Other grants	Remarks
1	2	3	4	5	6
	ed by direct payment of salary to private college staff and maintenance, contingency, library and laboratory grants have replaced the other grants envisaged in the grants-in-aid code.				remit them in a separate account in the name of the principal of the institution. The fees will be utilised only for the purpose for which they have been collected.
Maharashtra	The maintenance grant to a college should be equal to A *Minus* B. That is— (A) (i) entire establishment expenditure of the college during the year for which grants in paid *Plus* (ii) notional expenditure on normal maintenance and	As mentioned under maintenance grants.	-nil-		1. New college will not be paid grant for one year. 2. It should fulfil all conditions prescribed by the Government and the University. 3. From 1977, the government has introduced a salary payment scheme to ensure

1	2	3	4	5	6
	current repairs of the college building (ranging from 2% to 6% of the capital cost in inverse relation to the year of construction) or 75% of the expenditure on reasonable rent paid during the preceding year to the landlord and notional rent for the principals' residence, plus entire actual expenditure of the preceding year of the college on admissible items other than (i) and (ii) above subject to following ceilings: 18%, 15% and 12% of the admissible establishment expen-				full and regular payment of salary and allowances to college teachers. 4. It should have the following enrolments: 1 Single faculty colleges / 2 Double faculty colleges / 3 Triple faculty colleges
			1. Colleges in Municipal Corporation areas		300 / 500 / 700
			2. Colleges in town with a population of one lakh and above		200 / 350 / 500
			3. Colleges in town with less than one lakh population		100 / 175 / 250

State	Maintenance grants	Building/hostel grants	Equipment grants	Other grants	Remarks
1	2	3	4	5	6
	diture of the college of the preceding year respectively, if the college has only science faculty, is multi-faculty colleges with science faculty or is of Education, or purely arts or purely commerce subjects. *Minus* (B) (i) Tuition fees at approved rates recoverable by the college during the previous year. (ii) Surplus if any of the preceding year relating to the junior college classes attached to the college.				

1	2	3	4	5	6
Madhya Pradesh	75% of the gross admissible expenditure in the previous year or the net deficit, whichever is less plus 5% additional grant in the case of institutions of higher education. An additional 5% will be allowed in the non-assessment year following the assessment year.	*Building Grants*: (i) Institutions in urban areas: one-third of the total expenditure (urban areas: 10,000 or more population). (ii) Institutions in rural areas, girls' institutions and special institutions like music and arts, teacher training etc.: 50%.	50% on items other than science laboratories, fittings and 75% in case of science laboratories.	*Contingent Grants* (i) Building rent. (ii) Taxes on building @ Rs. 750. (iii) Repairs of buildings @ Rs. 3,750 for institutions with less than 1,500 students.	1. The institutions should have been in existence for at least one year prior to the date of application. 2. No grant, if the institution is found by the State Education department unnecessary or unsuited for the requirement of the locality. 3. The members of the staff will in no way associate themselves with political activity. 4. The management will reserve 15% and 18% teaching posts for Scheduled Castes and

State	Maintenance grants	Building/hostel grants	Equipment grants	Other grants	Remarks
1	2	3	4	5	6
					Scheduled Tribes respectively. 5. Grant shall be operative for two years at a time.
Nagaland	Ad hoc grants are given on the basis of request from the college giving particulars of enrolment, staff, income and expenditure. The actual quantum of grant is decided by a committee under the chairmanship of Education Minister and subject to availability of funds.				
Orissa	*Recurring:* (a) Colleges in advanced areas of the state receive 1/3rd of the net deficit as grant-in-aid	*Non-Recurring* (a) 50% of the estimated cost for buildings, equipments, books			Recurring Contingent Grant would be given @ Rs. 22- per student in arts/ commerce colleges

1	2	3	4	5	6
	after 5 years from the date of recognition, 2/3rd after 7 years and full net deficit after 9 years. Direct payment of salaries to both teaching and non-teaching staff would be applicable from the year (academic year starting from 1st June) the college is entitled to full net deficit-grant. (b) In backward areas, these periods shall be 3, 5 and 7 years instead of 5, 7 and 9 years respectively. (C.D. Block having half or less than half of the state average in literacy is to be treated as an educationally backward area). (c) The period in respect of women's	etc. for arts colleges. (b) 66-2/3 of the estimated cost in respect of buildings, equipments etc. for science colleges.			and Rs. 55/- per student in science colleges taking into account the actual enrolment subject to the condition that no contingent grant would be paid in respect of students enrolled as a result of inerease of seats, opening of new classes, till it qualifies to receive full deficit grant for the purpose.

State	Maintenance grants	Building/hostel grants	Equipment grants	Other grants	Remarks
1	2	3	4	5	6
	colleges shall be the same as prescribed for backward areas in (b) above. (d) Newly recognised colleges, which are entitled to receive grant-in-aid for the first time shall deposit their fees and fines in full only from the year their staff receives direct payment from Government.				
Punjab	Grants on the basis of 95% deficit are available for the following items. (i) Pay and allowances of teaching and non-teaching staff; (ii) contribution towards the provident fund of eligible employees.		Managements are to provide 1½ times the amount given by the Government. It is of a non-recurring character.		1. The grant will be available in respect of posts in existence on 1st November 1977, paid out of management fund. 2. The college must not allow its income from

1	2	3	4	5	6
					approved resource to fall below the level of such income during the financial year 1977-78. 3. The college would follow the rules of recruitment framed by the state government. The selection of teachers will be subject to confirmation by the Director of Public Instruction, Punjab. 4. Fees and funds shall be realised in accordance with the instructions issued by the university concerned from time to time.

State	Maintenance grants	Building/hostel grants	Equipment grants	Other grants	Remarks
1	2	3	4	5	6
Rajasthan	*Recurring Grants*:** Category A: 80% of the expenditure Category B: 70% of the previous Category C: 60% year plus likely Category D: 50% annual increment of staff. Exceptional category: 100% Special category: 90% Total grant will not exceed the deficit.	50%	Furniture and Equipment—50%	Bus—25%	The institution will be eligible for grant-in-aid only if it has existed for five years. There is a grant-in-aid Committee consisting of Director of Education, Chairman, Board of Secondary Education, Director of Technical Education etc.

Note : The total recurring grant shall not exceed the difference between the total approved expenditure and income from fees and other sources during the same year including grants from State and Central Government/ Sabhas, Societies and Local Bodies.

**The following will be the basis of categorisation of institutions: (i) Quality of educational work judged on the results on an average of last 3 years of public examinations of the highest class in institutions; (ii) Correction work; (iii) Individual attention; (iv) Teaching efficiency; (v) Discipline and tone of institution; (vi) Extra curricular activities; (vii) Contribution to community life; (viii) Class-wise attendance throughout the year; (ix) facilities for games, sports etc.; (x) Provision for building and equipment; (xi) Absence of malpractices and irregularities; (xii) Absence of stagnation among students; (xiii) number of faculties and subjects provided

1	2	3	4	5	6
	Special category institutions carrying on work of an experimental nature shall be entitled to 90% of the approved expenditure.				*Excess income from fees charged at higher rates than those in Government institutions shall be excluded from the income of the Institution.*
Tamil Nadu	*Teaching Grants*: 1. Grant paid @ 80% of net deficit over and above the fee income at management rates. 2. 100% grant for payment of DA sanctioned on or after 1-10-1973. 3. 100% grant for loss sustained on fee concession to Backward and Scheduled Caste classes and introduction of free PUC.	*Building Grants*: (Including purchase of land): 50% of the total cost subject to a maximum of Rs. 75,000 to first grade colleges and Rs. 50,000 to second grade colleges.	Grant for furniture, books and appliances: 50% of the total cost subject to a maximum of Rs. 10,000.		No private college shall levy any fee or collect any other charge or receive any other payment except a fee, charge or payment specified by the competent authority.

State	Maintenance grants	Building/hostel grants	Equipment grants	Other grants	Remarks
1	2	3	4	5	6
Tripura	90% of the difference between the approved expenditure on teachers' salaries and employees' contribution to provident fund and the income from fees and fines etc.	50% of the actual expenditure subject to a maximum of Rs. 2 lakhs.	50% of the total expenditure	Contingent grant to the extent of 90% of the actual expenditure subject to 1/6 of the expenditure on staff salaries.	1. The college should be affiliated to the University of Calcutta, should be well managed, maintain satisfactory discipline and accepted standard of academic efficiency. 2. It should be a non-profit making institution and be registered as a Society under the Societies Registration Act, 1860. 3. The college should have a regularly constituted managing body and qualified staff.

1	2	3	4	5	6
					4. It should have adequate income from endowments and other sources (excluding fees). 5. It should have adequate reserve fund. 6. It shall charge fees as prescribed by the Government for government colleges. 7. It should have adequate accommodation; at least 10 sq. ft. floor area per student.
Uttar Pradesh	From 31-3-1975 onwards, the state pays salary to the teachers in colleges on the colleges depositing 80% of the feeincome for the faculty		50% of the expenditure is provied as matching share for U.G.C. grants, to a few colleges, which are willing to take		1. Grant-in-aid will be available only after 5 years of establishment. 2. The institutions should not be

State	Maintenance grants	Building/hostel grants	Equipment grants	Other grants	Remarks
1	2	3	4	5	6
	of Arts and 75% for the faculty of science in the payment of Salary Account.		U.G.C. grants or spend at least 50% of the total expenditure from their own sources.		receiving grant-in-aid from the Central Government.
West Bengal	(i) *Maintenance Grants* Government Sponsored Colleges: The entire deficit on the approved items of expenditure on account of maintenance of the science colleges is met by the Government. (ii) *Private Colleges*: A lumpsum grant which covers 50% of deficit or Rs. 30,000, whichever is less. The	*For Men's colleges*: Government grant shall not ordinarily exceed the amount contributed from private sources. *For Women's Colleges*: Government grant shall not ordinarily exceed double the amount contributed from private sources.	*Equipment:* Grants are released in favour of deserving colleges subject to budget provision.		

1	2	3	4	5	6
	items covered are difference in UGC scales and College scales of pay and the D.A. to teaching and non-teaching staff.				

APPENDIX III—(contd.)

PATTERNS OF STATE GRANT-IN-AID FOR INSTITUTIONS OF TECHNICAL EDUCATION

State	Maintenance grants	Building grants	Equipment grants	Other grants	Remarks
1	2	3	4	5	6
Andhra Pradesh	*Boys' Polytechnics*: 65% of the gross expenditure to be met by the government; fees to be made over to the managements. *Girls' Polytechnics*: 80% of the gross expenditure to be met by government (no fees charged).	*Non-recurring expenditure*: Boys' Polytechnics: 25% of the cost (50% is met by the Central Government). *Girls Polytechnics*: 12½% of the cost (75% met by the Central Government).		No grants for non-recurring expenditure is being sanctioned as the colleges are having well established buildings.	
Assam	Regional Engineering College, Silchar, is eligible for 50% recurring and 100% for land and its development.	There is no private college in Assam and hence no grant in-aid rules have been prescribed.			

1	2	3	4	5	6
Bihar	No grant-in-aid admissible.				
Gujarat	90% of the admissible expenditure of Engineering colleges and polytechnics or the difference between the income and admissible expenditure, whichever is less. In the case of junior technical schools, this percentage is 50.	Central grants paid after the completion of the work.			Private institutions will be under the supervision of the department of Technical Education in respect of staff strength, salary scales, fees etc. The institutes may charge 50% higher rates of fees with the approval of the D.T.E. and still higher rates with the approval of the state government.
Haryana	No uniform pattern of assistance; the State Government gives grants				

State	Maintenance grants	Building grants	Equipment grants	Other grants	Remarks
1	2	3	4	5	6
	to private technical institutions for meeting recurring and nonrec-curring expenditure on the basis of provision made in the agreement signed with each insti-tutions. From 1-4-1976 the State Government has been giving, in res-pect of two private diploma institutions at Rohtak, 90% of the net deficit recurring expendi-ture and 25% non-recurring expenditure. In the case of Regional Engineering College, the Government meets 50% of the recurring deficit and entire expenditure on land and its development.				
Himachal Pradesh		No rules have been framed for grant-in-aid			

1	2	3	4	5	6
		to Technical Colleges/ Polytechnics.			
Jammu and Kashmir	The pattern of State Grant-in-aid is the same as for general education colleges.				
Karnataka	Maintenance Grants : 85% of the net deficit. *Loss of fee* income : Grant to cover loss of fee income at the rate of 100% at the management rates of fees.	Building grants. 50% of the total expenditure for the purchase of land, construction or extension of building, playgrounds, canteen building, cycle stand, staff quarters etc. subject to a financial limit of Rs. 50,000 per annuam to an institution. If, for want of funds,	Equipment grants : 50% of the total expenditure within a financial limit of Rs. 50,000 to an Engineering College and Rs, 20,000 to a polytechnic.	Benefit of Triple benefit scheme has been extended for private colleges/polytechnics in place of provident fund scheme.	1. No grant will be payable to an institution with a surplus or balance on hand of Rs. one lakh or more. 2. Institution should have average daily attendance of not less than 50% of the maximum strength of pupils.

State	Maintenance grants	Building grants	Equipment grants	Other grants	Remarks
1	2	3	4	5	6
		building grants cannot be given, loan may be given for the same purpose, subject to availability of funds.			
Kerala	Direct payment of salary by Government	*Building Grants** Central Govt: 50% State Govt: 25% Management: 25% *Maintenance Grants for buildings*; College: up to Rs, 30,000, polytechnics: up to Rs. 15,000.	*Workshop and Equipment Grants* a) College : Rs. 3,000; b) Polytechnic Rs. 1,000	*Laboratory* Colleges : Rs. 7,500, Polytechnic: Rs. 3,500 or actual net deficit expenditure. *Library Grants* College : Rs. 3,000; Polytechnics: Rs. 1,000 or actual net deficit.	*Grants for contingencies;* Colleges : up to Rs. 27,500, Polytechnics up to Rs. 17,500 *Student Tour Grants* A grant of Rs. 120 per final year student for engineering colleges and Rs. 60 per final year student for polytechnics plus extra expendi-

1	2	3	4	5	6
					ture on the TA/DA of staff members accompanying them.

*This holds good in the case of 6 out of 9 private institutions in the State. In the case of others, the State assistance is 1/6 for one and 25% for the other two institutions. The rest of the expenditure is to be shared by the Central Government and the management.

1	2	3	4	5	6
Madhya Pradesh	The grant-in-aid from the state government varies from institution to institution. For example, in the case of Madhav Engineering College, Gwalior, the society agreed to meet 50% of the approved non-recurring expenditure and also part of the recurring expenditure. In the case of Samrat Ashok Technological Institute, the society had agreed to pay 1/3 of the non-recurring				

State	Maintenance grants	Building grants	Equipment grants	Other grants	Remarks
1	2	3	4	5	6
	expenditure besides a sum of Rs. 5 lakhs for campus development.				
Maharashtra	*Maintenance Grants* : Colleges and Polytechnics; 90% of the admissible expenditure or the difference between their income and the admissible expenditure, whichever is less.		75% of the expenditure is borne by the State Government and 25% by the Management subject to approval of project report by the Government.	Expenditure on library, periodicals, reading rooms etc. will be as follows : Degree Courses: Rs. 70. Diploma Courses: Rs. 30 per student.	The scales of pay of teaching and non-teaching staff shall be the same as laid down by the Government from time to time.
Nagaland	Ad hoc grants are given to colleges on the basis of request from the college giving particulars of enrolment, staff, income and expenditure. The actual quantum of grant is decided by a committee under the Chairmanship of education minister				

1	2	3	4	5	6
	and subject to availability of funds.				
Orissa	50% of the recurring expenditure.	50% of the non-recurring expenditure.			
Punjab	Degree College: 75% of the deficit expenditure. Diploma Institutions: 90% of the deficit expenditure.	Automatic revision of pay scales/allowances with the revision in Government institutions.			
Rajasthan	As per pattern approved by Central Government and U.G.C.				
Tamil Nadu	Recurring Grants. 90% of the approved expenditure minus receipts.	Non-recurring (Buildings, Equipment, etc.) State Government 90%; Private			New development schemes : (purchase of new equipment, renewal of old and obsolete equipment, the

State	Maintenance grants	Building grants	Equipment grants	Other grants	Remarks
1	2	3	4	5	6
		Management 10% Within the ceilings fixed by the Southern Regional Committee of the All India Council for Technical Education.			pattern of assistance will be : State Government: 90% Management : 10%
Uttar Pradesh	The entire salary including allowances is payable from the State Revenues.			1. Rs. 165 per student on rolls is admissible as contingent grants. 2. Some lump-sum yearly grants are available for libraries, educational tours of students and the audit fees.	1. No grant is admissible to an institution before it completes 5 years of its existence. 2. The income of the institution from fees, hostels, interest, production centres is subtracted from the total grant payable to the insti-

1	2	3	4	5	6
					tution. The fee income is calculated after allowing for deduction for 15% full fee concession and 30% half freeships.
West Bengal	In the case of Polytechnics, the Government meets 100% grant after deducting income of the polytechnics from fees and Central Government sources.				

SELECT BIBLIOGRAPHY

Altekar, A.S., *Education in Ancient India*, Varanasi, 1965.

Ashby, Eric, *Universities: British, Indian and African*, London, 1966.

Association of Indian Universities: Higher Education and Development, New Delhi, 1975.

Azad, J.L., *Financing of Higher Education in India*, New Delhi, Sterling Publishers, 1975.

Azad, J.L., The Financing of Higher Education in India, Published in *Higher Learning in India*, Amrik Singh and Philip G. Altbach (Eds.), Vikas Publishing House, Delhi, 1974.

Azad, J.L., Government Grants for Higher Education: Preliminary Report, Planning Commission, New Delhi (Mimeo), 1975.

Baskin, Samuel, *Higher Education: Some Newer Developments*; New York, McGraw-Hill Company Inc., 1965.

Blaug, M., *Economics of Education*; Middlesex, England, Penguin Books, Vol. I, 1968; Vol. II, 1969.

Chambers, M.M., *Financing Higher Education*, Washington, 1963.

Goel, S.C., *Education and Economic Growth*, Macmillan Company, 1975.

Harris, Seymour E., *Higher Education in the United States: The Economic Problems*, Cambridge, Massachusetts, Harvard University Press, 1960.

Harris, Seymour E., *Financing of Higher Education*, New York, McGraw-Hill Book Company, Inc., 1959.

Harris, Seymour E., *Higher Education: Resources and Finance*, London, McGraw-Hill Book Company, Inc., 1962.

Joshi, K.L., *Problems of Higher Education in India: An Approach to Structural Analysis and Reorganisation*, 1979.

Joshi, K.L., *Higher Educatian, Historical and other Problems*, Popular Prakashan, Bombay, 1981.

Misra, A.N., *Financing Education in India*, Allahabad, Garg Brothers, 1959.

Misra, A.N., *Educational Finance in India*, Bombay, Asia Publishing House, 1962.

Misra, A.N., *The Financing of Indian Education*, Bombay, Asia Publishing House, 1967.

Mitra, Ved, *Education in Ancient India*, New Delhi, 1964.

Mookerjee, R.K., *Ancient Indian Education*, London, 1951.

Myrdal, Gunnar, *Asian Drama*, New York, 1968.

Naik, J.P., *Educational Planning in India*, Banaras, Allied Publishers, 1965.

Naik, J.P., Central Assistance for General Education Colleges: Existing and Proposed, Education Commission, Government of India, Mimeo, 1965.

Naik, J.P., Grant-in-aid to Educational Institutions in India, Education Commission, Government of India, New Delhi, Mimeo, 1965.

Naik, J.P., The Role of Private Enterprise in Education, Education Commission, Government of India, Mimeo, 1965.

Naik, J.P., *Education for our People*, Allied Publishers, 1978.

Nallagounden, A.M., *Education and Development*, Ph.D. thesis, Mimeo, 1965.

Nanjundappa, D.M.. *Working of University Finances*, Sterling Publishers, 1976.

Organization of European Community and Development (OECD), Study Group on the Economics of Education: Economic Aspects of Higher Education, Germany, Organisation for Economic Cooperation and Development, 1966.

— Financing of Education for Economic Growth, Paris, 1966.

— Efficiency in Resource Utilisation on Education, Paris, 1969.

— The Residual Factor and Economic Growth, Paris, 1964.

— Social Objectives in Educational Planning, Paris, 1967.

Panchmukhi, P.R. *Economic of University Finances*, Dharwar, 1977.

Panchmukhi, P.R., *Education and Research in Economics*, Bombay, 1973.

Panchmukhi, P.R., Measurement of the Effects of Public Expenditure—Ph.D. thesis, Bombay University, Bombay 1967.

Pfnister Allan O., *Planning for Higher Education*, Westview Press, Colorado, 1976.

Rao, V.K.R.V., *Education and Human Resource Development*, New Delhi, 1966.

Rao, V.K.R.V., *University Education and Employment*, Bombay.

Sharma, G.D., *Enrolment in Higher Education*, New Delhi, 1977.

Sharma, G.D., *Resource Allocation on Education*, New Delhi, 1978.

Singh, Amrik, ed., *The Higher Learning in India*, Vikas, 1974.

Thompson, Kennethw, *et. al.*, *Higher Education and Social Change*, New York, 1977.

UNESCO, *Access to Higher Education*, Paris, 1965.

UNESCO, *Economic and Social Aspects of Educational Planning*, Paris, 1965.

UNESCO, *Financing of Education*, Paris, 1965.

UNESCO, *Readings in the Economics of Education*, Paris, 1968.

UNESCO, *Statistical Year Book*, Paris, 1968.

UNESCO, *World Survey of Education*, III, Secondary Education, Paris, 1966.

UNESCO, *World Survey of Education*, IV, Higher Education, Paris. 1966.

Vaizey, John, *The Costs of Education*, London, George Allen and Unwin Ltd., 1958.

Vaizey, John, *The Economics of Education*, London, Faber and Faber, 1962.

Vaizey, John, *Education in Modern World*, World University Library, London, Weidenfeld and Nicolson, 1967.

Higher Education, *Who Pays, Who Benefits, Who Should Pays*? The Cannegie Commission for Higher Education, McGraw-Hill, 1975.

REPORTS/GOVERNMENT PUBLICATIONS

— Report of the Education Commission, 1964-66.
— A Report on Social Sciences in India, Retrospective and Prospective, ICSSR, Review Committee, 1973.
— Report of the Second Review Committee, ICSSR, New Delhi, 1978.
— Report of Committee on Colleges, U.G.C., New Delhi, 1967.
— Report of the Review Committee of the UGC, New Delhi, 1977.
— Report of the Review Committee on Agricultural Universities, ICAR, New Delhi, 1978.
— Report of the University Education Commission, 1948-49, New Delhi, 1962.
— Annual Reports of University Grants Commission.
— Annual Reports of the Ministry of Education.
— Draft National Policy on Education, Ministry of Education, New Delhi, 1979.
— Planning Commission: Five Year Plans, Annual Plans, Progress Reports.
— Centre for Monitoring Indian Economy, Basic Statistics Relating to the Indian Economy, Vol. I, All India, Bombay, 1977.
— Vol. II—States, Bombay, 1977.
— C.S.O., Basic Statistics Relating to Indian Economy, 1950-51 to 1975-76, New Delhi.
— Ministry of Education:
  — Education In India.
  — Education in States of India.
  — Education in Universities in India.
— State Governments:
  — Grant-in-aid Rules/Codes/Government Orders issued from time to time.

REPORTS/GOVERNMENT PUBLICATIONS

Report of the Education Commission, 1964-66.

A Report on Social Sciences in India, Recommendations and Directory, Social Science Committee, 1973.

Report of the Second Review Committee, ICSSR, New Delhi, 1978.

Report of the Committee on [illegible], ICSSR, New Delhi, 197[illegible].

Report of the Review Committee of the ICAR, New Delhi, 1972.

Report of the Review Committee on Agricultural Universities, ICAR, New Delhi, 1978.

Report of the University Education Commission, 1948-49, New Delhi, 1949.

Annual Reports of University Grants Commission.

Annual Reports of the Ministry of Education.

Draft National Policy on Education, Ministry of Education, New Delhi, 1979.

Planning Commission: Five Year Plans, Annual Plans, Progress Reports.

Centre for Monitoring Indian Economy, Basic Statistics relating to the Indian Economy, Vol. II, All India, Bombay, 197[illegible].

[illegible] 1977.

CSO, Basic Statistics Relating to Indian Economy, 1950-51 to 1975-76, New Delhi.

Ministry of Education:

— Education in India.

— Education in States of India.

— Education in Universities in India.

State Government:

— [illegible] Government Orders, [illegible].

Index